CLOISTERS
OF EUROPE

CLOISTERS
OF EUROPE
GARDENS OF PRAYER

PHOTOGRAPHS BY DANIEL FAURE
TEXT BY VÉRONIQUE ROUCHON MOUILLERON

Translated from the French by Deke Dusinberre

VIKING STUDIO

CONTENTS

HORTUS CONCLUSUS

Cloister: in the broadest sense, "cloister" refers to an entire monastery, a place where a Christian community lives in deliberate isolation. It suggests the very idea of enclosure, of secluded life. In a stricter sense, cloister is an architectural term referring to an enclosed courtyard formed by the walls of a church and its residential buildings, ringed by a covered colonnade that overlooks the central quadrangle. Both concepts are conveyed by a single word in English and French (*cloître*), whereas German, for instance, distinguishes between the two (*Kloster* and *Kreuzgang*).

Cloisters were basically a medieval artistic phenomenon that flourished in Western Europe between the eighth and fifteenth centuries. They are thus linked to medieval forms of Western Christianity not only from the standpoint of institution and structure but also in terms of devotional role. Hence from the eleventh century onward, this architectural feature, first adopted by monks, was imitated by "canons regular" (priests who lived by their church, in a community governed by a rule). Monastic cloisters, generally built in the calm expanse of the countryside far from cities, thereby found an echo in cloisters for the canonry, often located in the center of town, alongside the canons' cathedral or church.

Whether monastic or canonical, a cloister always entailed a patio, an open quadrangle in which flowers or bushes were often planted, arranged around a fountain or well. Medieval Latin therefore called it the *hortus conclusus*, "enclosed garden." This poetic nickname was also a spiritual image, a horticultural metaphor for souls consecrated to God. The amorous Biblical hymn known as the Song of Solomon notably described the Beloved as a secret orchard, "a garden enclosed, a fountain sealed" (4:12). Like the other erotic metaphors in the Song of Solomon, this *hortus conclusus* is ambivalent; it should not be interpreted solely as an image of virginity or bodily chastity, but also as a declaration of total, exclusive love between the soul and its Divine Beloved. The cloister, as *hortus conclusus*, therefore embodied both a material, architectural reality and a spiritual, Christian ideal of religious life.

Most of the major medieval cloisters have been deconsecrated and are no longer closed to visitors, who can now walk around them freely, marveling at refined arches, deciphering scenes carved into capitals, and generally admiring a cloister as a fine artistic object. Yet in order to understand the rationale behind its architecture, the inspiration behind its decoration, and the way its carvings should be interpreted, the people who once populated that cloister must be brought back to life.

The lives of those clerics were firmly rooted in a daily discipline based—especially for monks and nuns—on strict rules that orchestrated the entire day. This book will therefore strive to present cloisters as an everyday living environment, a place where monks and canons were regularly to be found, the site of their practical and spiritual activities.

A review of monastic and canonical practices—how they evolved from the Carolingian period to the late Middle Ages—will thus revivify the architectural setting of a cloister, rescuing it from certain death. Upon this very concrete and occasionally anecdotal foundation, the spiritual significance of the cloister will then be discussed, based on medieval chroniclers such as Hugo de Folieto, Honorius Augustodunensis, and William Durandus of Mende. It was simultaneously a functional space and the reflection of a contemplative soul, where every element was interpreted in a symbolic light. Everything was full, almost bursting with meaning—allegorical, typological, didactic, and moral. This spiritual interpretation sheds light on the figurative decoration of cloisters during the Romanesque era, just as it explains the later rejection of that decoration in the writings of Bernard of Clairvaux: in Cistercian—and, later, Gothic—architecture, the meditative gazes of monks were nourished solely on repetitive patterns of stone where light and shadow played freely. The final part of this book will return to "historiated" Romanesque cloisters—those with figures or stories sculpted into columns and capitals—and will study the main motifs that appear there. Thanks to these visual details, which allude directly to the activities of its pious residents, a cloister can become a theater concretely evoking medieval monks and canons—it once again becomes a real, live place.

SAINT-MARTIN-DU-CANIGOU (FRANCE).

MONKS AND MONASTERIES

EREMITIC OR CENOBITIC

A monk, as the word's Greek root suggests (*monos*, alone), is a solitary figure, withdrawn from the world and from everything "secular." The first monastic experiments were conducted in the early fourth century in the Orient, notably in Egypt between Thebes and the Nile delta. That was home to Anthony and Pachomius, the great inventors and true founders of Eastern monasticism. Very soon two different types of monastic life coexisted, one called eremitic (from *eremos*, desert) and the other labeled cenobitic (from *koinos* and *bios*, life in common). An eremitic monk—or hermit—lived in the desert like Anthony, in complete solitude and total asceticism, alone with God yet also alone with the temptations of mind and body. Such a recluse therefore had to be heroic, a true "athlete" of the faith, in order to avoid succumbing to madness or to the vanity of his mortifications. Since not all monks were capable of joining this spiritual elite, and because other Christian values were worth cultivating, Pachomius instituted the principles of a cenobitic life: monks were expected to live in a community, to submit to a set of regulations (or "rule") and to the hierarchical and spiritual authority of an abbot (a term derived from the Aramaic word *abba*, father).

The fourth and fifth centuries spawned many monastic experiments in East and West, notably conducted by Jerome, Augustine of Hippo in North Africa, Martin of Tours, Honoratus, Caesarius of Arles, and Cassian of Provence. In the East, however, one figure surpassed all others in the resonance his rule had on Greek and Slavic monasticism in the Middle Ages—Basil of Caesarea, who died in 379 and who reinforced the Pachomian principles of the unity of monks and their obedience to an abbot. In the West, it was Benedict of Nursia who received the lofty title of "the father of

Western monasticism." Benedict apparently lived between 490 and 560, having been born in Umbria. He first went to Rome, then moved to Subiaco, later continuing southward toward Monte Cassino where he founded his main monastery sometime around 530. Although Benedict was buried at Monte Cassino, due to Lombard pillaging in the late sixth century his remains were allegedly translated with great piety to France, to an abbey at Fleury (now named, after Benedict, Saint-Benoît-sur-Loire).

THE SLOW RISE OF THE BENEDICTINE RULE

By Benedict's own admission, his rule was just a modest beginning, a "little rule . . . for beginners" (*Rule of Saint Benedict*—hereafter RB—73:8). Why was the Benedictine Rule so influential when, in the mid sixth century, it was just one monastic code among many that flourished at the time? It was fairly brief, divided into a prologue and seventy-three chapters, and was composed for the use of the Monte Cassino monastery, with no thought to wider diffusion. And we now know that it was directly based on a long, highly similar but anonymous text known as the "Rule of the Master." Benedict also drew on the writings of Cassian (founder of Saint-Victor in Marseilles), Augustine, Pachomius, Basil, and Caesarius, respecting the pattern of the major Eastern and Western cenobitic traditions. Yet the intrinsic qualities of his rule set it apart from its sources. Its most notable quality is the measured and practical tone that governs the requirements of monastic life. During an epoch that felt it was past its prime, when the heroism of hermits was no longer appropriate, a monk's salvation required another type of self-denial—the denial of his individual will. This meant submitting to the abbot's and Christ's will, becoming completely one with the community around the abbot, seeking to alter his ways—with and through the other monks—in matters of charity, humility, and work, and promising to honor the rule and to remain at the monastery until death. Such asceticism included renouncing personal property and accepting chastity, periods of fasting, and manual labor, but the practice of extreme mortification was rejected in favor of reasonable requirements. The life of a monk—to be discussed more fully below—was organized around the twin poles of prayer and work, as defined by the rule down to the tiniest details. The special qualities of the Benedictine Rule were fraternal obedience and charity, disciplinary moderation and realism. They explain, in part, why it was adopted by many communities starting in the late sixth century, a period when the abbey at Monte Cassino was nevertheless emptied and ruined by Lombard invasions. It was therefore not until the ninth century that this rule triumphed over all others, playing an exclusive role in Western monasticism.

BENEDICT AND COLUMBANUS

Prior to the ninth century, monks often adopted a composite constitution by combining various customs. Each monastery was autonomous and could issue its own rule, provided that the community adhered to it. Initially, the Benedictine Rule simply complemented other rules, notably that of Saint Columbanus (c. 540–615). Columbanus represented the other path of Western monasticism, which originated in Ireland and was rooted in Celtic Christianity. Columbanus left Ireland for the continent, moving from northern France to the Rhineland and on to Lombardy. With his disciples, this Irish monk founded many abbeys along the way, from Luxeuil in the Vosges region to Jouarre in Brie, and from Saint Gall on Lake Constance to Bobbio in the Apennines, where he died. It is worth noting that Columbanus's Rule stressed corporal punishment and penitence; there was a real attachment to the cenobitic life, but the rule of strict obedience and subordination to the abbot was more important than horizontal relationships to other monks. Furthermore, the Irish monks were often priests at the same time, and they sought to go out and evangelize the world whereas in the original Benedictine ideal (which would soon evolve) prospective monks were laymen seeking their own salvation within closed walls. Although Columbanus's Rule made the spiritual goals of monastic life clear, it was much less specific about details of daily activities than was Benedict's Monte Cassino constitution. That is why most monastic houses in the seventh and eighth centuries adopted a mixed Columbano–Benedictine rule.

THE TWO BENEDICTS

The equilibrium between the two rules was broken—in favor of the Benedictines—by the conversion of Germany in the eighth century. That task was accomplished by Anglo-Saxon monks led by Saint Boniface (died 754), who founded the powerful abbey at Fulda and was dubbed the "Apostle of Germania." These English monks followed the Benedictine Rule for two reasons: southern England was evangelized, on the orders of Pope Gregory the Great (590–604), by Italian Benedictines from the abbey of Sant' Andrea in Rome with their prior, Augustine (who became the first archbishop of Canterbury); furthermore, political and liturgical motives led the authorities to favor the Anglo-Saxon clergy from Augustine's houses over Celtic monks who had spread across northern Britain and Ireland (664). In Germany, at Boniface's urging, monasteries (headed by Fulda) therefore adopted the Benedictine system. This tendency was then strongly reinforced by successive Frankish kings—Pepin the Short (c. 715–768), Charlemagne (747–814), and Louis

the Pious (778–840)—who sought to unify the kingdom politically and religiously.

During the synods of 816, 817, and 818, held at Aachen in the reign of Louis the Pious, bishops and abbots officially decided that all monks in the new "Holy Roman Empire" should follow the same Benedictine system. Monastic capitularies (or ordinances) were issued to restate the goals of renouncing the world, of asceticism, and of communal work and prayer. The capitularies also laid down a few practical measures concerning a monk's timetable and the election of abbots. One man used all his influence on Emperor Louis to obtain these measures, which changed the course of Western monasticism: Benedict of Aniane. Born to a Visigoth family, originally named Witiza, the young man was raised at the Carolingian court and destined for a career as an imperial civil servant until he renounced the worldly life and fully adopted the Benedictine model, taking on the name of Benedict himself. At Aniane, in what is now southern France, he founded a monastery where the rule was strictly applied. As a close and faithful adviser to Emperor Louis, Benedict was behind the promulgations of 816–817, as well as several corrections and adaptations of Benedict of Nursia's original text. After four centuries of varied monastic experiments, the era of Benedictine unity was born—*una regula, una consuetudo*: "one rule, one custom."

CLUNY

The broad acceptance of the Benedictine Rule and the founding of Benedictine houses generated by the monastic charters of 816–817 should not, however, be misconstrued. The political instability of the Carolingian empire and the shock of invasions (Norsemen from the west, Hungarians from the east, Saracens from the south) led to secular and ecclesiastic interference, to worldly intrusion, to a slackening of dis-

SAINT-MICHEL-DE-CUXA (FRANCE).

cipline, and to an instability little suited to the monastic life envisaged by the two Benedicts. That is why it seemed necessary, as early as the tenth century, to reinvigorate Benedictine establishments. Many monks undertook this task in the Paris region, in Lorraine, in the Rhineland and elsewhere, but history has primarily credited the Benedictine revival to the site of Cluny with its famous line of abbots: Odo (abbot 927–942) and Mayeul (954–994) in the tenth century, followed by Odilo (994–1049) and Hugh of Semur (1049–1109), whose two abbacies spanned the entire eleventh century. The abbots' reforming efforts enabled them to build an entire network of close ties to monasteries all across Europe, whereas other Benedictine abbeys had merely accomplished local, isolated reform. A Cluniac abbot traveled constantly, working to have his rule and customs adopted by the monasteries he visited, even luring monks desirous of reform away from communities that rejected it. Cluny's itinerant action helped it to establish a veritable, uniform monastic empire, carefully structured and governed, independent of both the temporal power of lords and the ecclesiastic jurisdiction of bishops—for Cluny answered directly to Rome, enjoying exclusive links to the papacy. The Cluniac family was organized hierarchically around the mother house of Cluny itself; first came priories, which had no abbot at their head and depended directly on the mother house; then there were daughter houses, whose abbots were subject to the centralized authority of the "arch-abbot" of Cluny; finally, there were affiliated abbeys, which adopted the Cluniac reform but maintained their autonomy vis-à-vis Cluny. At its height, around 1100, Cluny could be described as a veritable church within the Church, *Ecclesia cluniacensis*—an order of monk-priests that was highly influential with the pope and ecclesiastic authorities, a rich congregation known for its magnificent buildings, artworks, and liturgy.

SANTO DOMINGO DE SILOS (SPAIN).

BLACK MONKS, WHITE MONKS

At the dawn of the twelfth century, Western monasticism was therefore generally Benedictine or Benedictine-like, and could be divided into two broad groups—Cluniac and non-Cluniac. Although Cluny's pyramidal, tentacular empire was striking, it should not be forgotten that the majority of Benedictine monasteries were not a part of it. Since these latter monasteries had no specific ties and were scattered from England to Italy and from Mont-Saint-Michel (France) to Hirsau (Swabia), they had no combined power.

In the late eleventh century there nevertheless arose a movement within the Benedictine family that would spread and take root everywhere, directly competing with Cluny (despite differing structures), finally surpassing Cluniac establishments in number and influence. The movement began in Cîteaux, where Robert de Molesme founded a new monastery in 1098. Yet it was thanks to Bernard of Clairvaux—Saint Bernard (1090–1153)—that the Cistercian movement really took off, starting in 1113. Cistercians (i.e., from Cîteaux) were Benedictine reformers who advocated a stricter reading of Saint Benedict; like all medieval Christian reforms, the Cistercian reform viewed itself as a return to roots, to original purity. Cistercians felt that Cluny in particular had gradually undermined the Rule's requirements through an accumulation of overly lax practices. Cluniac monks lived in a more worldly way, like feudal lords; completely taken up with the divine liturgy, they were granted special dispensations in terms of work and food as compensation for singing all those long and wonderful services, or for saying the many private masses held several times a day on various altars.

Cistercians sought to re-establish what they saw as a more harmonious balance between Benedict's two mainstays of monastic life: prayer and manual labor. Austerity, asceticism, and isolation were their principle guidelines. That explains the Cistercian organization's founding of vast, isolated monastic estates that rendered the monks almost completely self-sufficient. It also explains the order's use of "lay brothers" who dedicated their lives to God and lived with the monks in order to perform certain tasks, but who did not observe the Rule. Their role was to enable the "choir monks" (who were also priests) to perform the holy service. In addition to the numerous daughter houses established by Cîteaux, the movement was joined by a great number of existing houses that remained autonomous even though highly attached—spiritually and emotionally—to the mother house and father-abbot. Cistercians wore a white habit, as distinct from the black habit worn by Cluniacs and all other Benedictines.

WHAT ABOUT WOMEN?

The spread of convents in the Middle Ages is poorly documented, and at any rate appears to have been much less extensive—in number and wealth—than its monastic model. Strict cloistering seems to have been the basic requirement of female religious life, clearly accompanied by a vow of stability (i.e., permanent attachment). Unlike monks who, starting in the eleventh century, combined monastic commitment with priestly status, nuns remained dependent on priests for the performing of sacraments, the saying of mass, and spiritual guidance. That is why convents were often founded at a later period, based on a Cluniac, Cistercian, or Carthusian monastery. Nuns had to seek the spiritual and jurisdictional guidance of monk-priests. Abbot Hugh of Cluny organized a major convent for Cluniac nuns at Marcigny-sur-Loire (France) in 1061. Many convents adopted Cistercian customs and asked to be affiliated to Saint Bernard's order. It should be noted however that monks were often reticent to accept this major and apparently risky responsibility, limiting it as much as possible. In the twelfth century there were a few exceptional cases of autonomous convents, just as there were "double monasteries" in which two communities, male and female, were founded together (and, at Fontevraud, even governed by an abbess); furthermore, the Paraclete congregation, founded by Héloise with advice from Abelard, depended on no specific male order.

BENEDICT OR BRUNO?

Cîteaux was emblematic of a broad movement of Benedictine reform, if different from—indeed rival to—Cluniac reform. Yet even prior to Cîteaux, there were other, less famous eleventh-century foundations whose reformist aspirations notably advocated complete isolation from the world. Some still considered themselves Benedictine (Savigny, Chaise-Dieux, and Regensburg around 1090), while others were distantly related to the Benedictine tradition while borrowing elements from Oriental desert monasticism, returning to an eremitical or semi-eremitical lifestyle (notably the Camaldolese order in Tuscany).

In the end, all those eremitical experiments, however original they may have been, clearly displayed Benedictine influence. Only the movement dubbed Carthusian (i.e., from Chartreuse) could be said to have devised a totally new constitution. Apart from a few practical regulations that reflect Saint Benedict's Rule, Carthusian life was largely alien to the Benedictine model. Carthusians wore white habits but were distinguished from other monks by their beards, in imitation of the earliest hermits and Camaldolese monks. The rule drawn up by Guigo I, who was prior from 1109 to 1136, reflects the aspirations of the movement's founder, Saint Bruno of Cologne. Originally a priest and canon at Reims, Bruno relinquished his post and with six companions founded a hermitage in 1084 in the rugged hills of La Grande-Chartreuse in southeastern France. Solitude and contemplation dominated the Carthusian lifestyle. The solitude was not only that of a monastery lost in the wilderness of an Alpine valley, but also that of an individual cell within the monastery. The hermitage was composed of a small garden and a few rooms where a monk ate, slept, prayed, studied, and did manual work. Monks met only rarely—each monk ate alone in his *cubiculum*, except on Sundays and feast days. He also prayed alone, except for mass and an early morning and evening service when he would go to church. A Carthusian monk who spent most of his time alone in a hermit's cell could not be said to lead a cenobitic life. In order to fulfill their hermit's calling, such monks were relieved of material obligations by lay brothers who lived somewhat apart in the "lower house" (called *La Correrie*) and formed their own, cenobitic, religious community more open to the world.

Not to be confused with monastic orders—and therefore to be discussed separately later—were orders of canons regular (which became widespread during the eleventh century) and mendicants (which emerged in the early thirteenth century). Although such orders followed a rule and organized their buildings around a cloister, they were not composed of monks who opted for solitude. Canons were above all priests who served a parish and had the cure of souls. Nor did mendicants reject the world, for they were completely involved with people and pastoral work; strictly speaking, they were mendicant friars, and it was only later that mendicants could become monks.

This chapter therefore concludes in 1215, the year of the Fourth Lateran Council, when Pope Innocent III decreed that no new monastic order would henceforth be admitted and recognized. Any new monastic order had to adhere to one of the existing rules, which it might enrich or purify but from which it must depend. This decision confirmed and insured the primacy, among Western monks, of the Benedictine system.

FONTENAY (FRANCE).

Between the ninth and sixteenth centuries, the siting and layout of cloisters changed very little. Cloisters constituted a generally stable architectural space—variants and modifications down through centuries had more to do with local constraints (topographical or climatic) than with any profound reform in religious lifestyle. The most numerous examples date from the twelfth and thirteenth centuries, and clearly display the broad lines of every cloister's organization. It was a quadrangle (or trapezoid) set against the north or south wall of the church, the other three sides being bounded by standard monastic buildings: the east wing, built as a two-story extension of the transept of the church, contained the monks' dormitory upstairs and the chapter-house downstairs; the wing parallel to the church housed the refectory; the west wing was used as a juncture to the exterior (perhaps giving on to the storerooms or, depending on period and monastic congregation, leading to a wing for guests or lay brothers). A staircase from the monks' dormitory led directly into the church; sometimes, a second stairway led down to the cloister. The kitchens were next to the refectory. Other rooms with specific functions, such as the monks' common room and the calefactory (or "warming room") might also be included in the overall design.

This type of plan was developed for abbeys adhering to the Order of Saint Benedict. The Benedictine system being the sole type of Western monasticism from the ninth to twelfth centuries, it is hardly surprising that this model was reproduced everywhere. The amazing thing, however, is that this same layout was adopted by other religious groups, whether monastic or not: by the eremitical monks of La Grande-Chartreuse (founded in 1084),

SÉNANQUE (FRANCE).

by canons living in their parish churches, and by the mendicant orders that sprang up in the thirteenth century. Was this imitation due to the matchless perfection of a powerful model, or to an extreme desire for standardization, or to the lazy repetition of a common pattern? Whatever the case, such cloisters were emblematic of the uniformity of medieval architecture.

THE BENEDICTINE PATTERN

The plan of Saint-Gall

Cloisters appeared during the Carolingian period. The plan of the abbey of Saint Gall (or Sankt Gallen) in Switzerland, built around 820, provides the earliest detailed illustration. This priceless document, an original parchment some 30 by 45 inches (77 cm. x 112 cm.), is currently preserved at the Saint Gall library (Stifts-bibliothek, Ms. 1092). The overall plan of the monastery is drawn in red ink, while many captions in black ink indicate the use of each building. It is thought to have been sent by Heito (died 823), abbot of Reichenau and bishop of Basel, to Gozbert, abbot of Saint Gall (816–836), who wanted to rebuild his abbey. The plan probably represents an idealized blueprint on more than one level, not only because it was never built as such at Saint Gall and because it combines a functional and symbolic perfection not previously found elsewhere, but also because this architectural plan is a thinly disguised theoretical reflection on monastic life. It must be related to the synods held at Aachen in 816–817 where, at the urging of Benedict of Aniane, the Benedictine Rule was extended to all monasteries. This legislation is thought to have been concretely accompanied by a model plan of a Benedictine abbey, of which the Saint Gall example may be the original or one of perhaps dozens of copies dispatched to the four corners of the Carolingian empire.

Although hardly created from thin air—since it clearly perfected earlier architectural experiments—the Saint Gall plan represented the veritable birth of Benedictine cloisters. Church and cloister joined at the south wall of the church, forming the vital core of monastic space (see illustration on page 182). The cloister's perfect square was bisected by four median paths that met in the middle, at a bush bearing red berries. The arrangement of the main buildings shown here would be respected for several centuries—the upper floor of the east wing was allocated to the dormitory (seventy-seven beds can be counted), at the far end of which the latrines are clearly drawn, linked by a corridor with a sharp bend designed to slow the progress of fumes. This plan was therefore functional as well as ideal, and was intended for flesh-and-blood users, honoring the concrete objectives of Benedict's rule. The ground floor of the east wing was a large room, not explicitly identified here as the chapter-house; the plan does note, however, that it was heated (the only warm room in the entire cloister). Bath and laundry room were connected by another corridor. The two floors of the south wing housed the refectory downstairs and a clothes room upstairs. Another corridor, also with a bend to minimize odors, led to the kitchen, which in turn led to the bakery and brewery. The west wing contained a downstairs cellar where rows of large and small casks (or the supports to hold them) can be clearly seen; upstairs was a storehouse. The parlor, wedged between the cellar and the wall of the church, represented the only link to the outside world—there monks could talk (*parler*) to guests or issue orders for the proper running of agricultural and craft operations. Except for this passage and the staircase leading into the church, the space of the cloister was totally self-enclosed.

On the Saint Gall plan, the southern gallery of the cloister alongside the church is the only specified meeting place for monks, where benches were probably installed. Chapter-houses were perhaps not systematically located on the ground floor of the east wing until the eleventh century. The chapter-house played a major role in the life of monks; along with the church, it was the other main space for shared events. The monks met there every day to read out loud one "chapter" of the monastic rule, which explains its name (in Latin it was also called *conventus*—gathering—which metonymically evolved into the term "convent"). The chapter-house had two other official functions—questions of internal governance were discussed there, and public penitence was performed there.

Cluny II

Once numerous architectural variants of the ninth and tenth centuries had been discarded, the Saint Gall pattern resurfaced at Cluny. The Cluniac determination to complete the Benedictine reform begun by the Carolingians probably explains this revival of the plan developed at Aachen. Cluny was marked by three successive building campaigns: its founding in 910, its enlargement in 981 (called Cluny II), and its extravagant extension from 1088 onwards, making the abbey the largest building in Western Christendom (Cluny III). Modern visitors to the site now see just ten percent of the original complex, all that remains of Cluny.

Excavations and descriptions in the book of customs written under Abbot Odilo (994–1049) enable us to say that the cloister of Cluny II mirrored the Carolingian model. Henceforth, underneath the immense dormitory with its ninety-seven beds, the ground floor of the east wing (which had been a single multipurpose hall in Saint Gall) was divided into the chapter-house and the parlor (*locutorium*). In the south wing, the refectory occupied both floors, but was slightly truncated to leave space for the warming room next door in the southeast corner, preserving the principle of a single heated room. The cellar and narrow corridor to the "almonry" (where alms were

distributed) occupied the west wing. On the other side of the refectory was a cloister for novices, imitating the cloister for professed monks but organized in a different, more limited way, since there was no need to repeat certain zones such as the church and chapter-house. Cluny thus provided the model for double-cloister complexes, although only the main cloister was organized according to the complete and henceforth standard system, occasionally called the "Benedictine pattern."

Cistercian cloisters

The Cistercian reform also left its mark on cloisters in two main ways: through its systematic, almost canonical allocation of the main and secondary rooms, and through its innovative establishment of a wing for lay brethren. This wing corresponded to the cellar side, that is to say the west gallery of the quadrangle. The presence within the monastery of lay brothers (who, it will be recalled, carried out the abbey's productive operations even as they had to attend certain services within the church) meant that they had to be kept apart from the cloistered space whose quiet could not be disturbed. Lay brothers could not go through the cloister, but had to take a walled corridor, called "lay-brother alley," that ran along the west wing now named after them. This meant that two galleries of a Cistercian cloister had no rooms behind them; one ran along the wall of the church, the other along the wall of lay-brother alley. Monastic buildings were concentrated in the monks' wings: upstairs were still the dormitory and latrines, downstairs were the sacristy and *armarium* (or library), chapter-house, stairway leading to the dormitory, passage traversing the whole wing, parlor, and common room (for various activities). The adjoining wing contained the refectory, warming room, and kitchen. Next to one of the galleries, in the courtyard, was a covered special lavabo (or stone washbasin) for the monks' ablutions.

In its broad lines, then, Saint Gall's Carolingian plan was adopted with remarkable unanimity down through the entire Middle Ages. The reasons for its popularity

Santa María de Poblet (Spain).

14

still are not understood, except that it was an integral part of a cenobitic lifestyle. The Carthusian model further reinforced this idea—Carthusian architecture was organized around two poles, one for solitary life and the other for community life (limited, as noted above, to a strict minimum). This led to at least two cloisters, although they no longer reflected the distinction between professed monks and novices as found in Benedictine abbeys. For the Carthusians, the large or main cloister was the quadrangle around which were aligned individual hermit cells for the monks, who would pass through it on their rare outings; it thereby illustrated the Carthusian ideal of a monastery of hermits living together in proximity yet alone. But as soon the need arose for communal space for prayers, meetings, or meals, the Benedictine architectural model returned to the fore—a second, or small, cloister was flanked by church, chapter-house, and refectory.

A cloister was the prerogative of monastic life, even more so than the church that monks might share with lay people. The plan of a cloister embodied the all-encompassing aspirations of monastic rules insofar as the quadrangle was designed to unite *spiritus* (the abbey church), *anima* (the chapter-house and other rooms related to intellectual work), and *corpus* (refectory, dormitory, warming room). As the pivotal site of passage and encounter, the cloister was the architectural emblem of cenobitic life.

CLOISTER CUSTOMS

The year according to Benedict

"Idleness is the enemy of the soul. Therefore the brothers should have specified periods for manual labor as well as for prayerful reading," wrote Benedict in chapter 48 of his Rule (RB 48: 1). Prayer and work were imperative, summed up by the famous Latin rhyme, *ora et labora*. For Benedict, these two occupations were not left to a monk's free will, to be decided on the spur of the moment, but had to be fixed and "regular"—based on a

<small>FONTFROIDE (FRANCE).</small>

rule in the fullest sense of the word.

The day was organized around church services, called divine offices, each lasting from half-an-hour to one-and-three-quarter hours. The entire community entered the church via the cloister (in daytime) or the dormitory staircase (at night), and would then sing psalms or, according to the rule's precise guidelines, hymns, *Gloria* and *Kyrie*. There were seven daytime offices, or "hours": at daybreak (around 4 or 5 a.m.) came Matins (or Lauds), followed at 6 a.m. by Prime (the "first hour" of the day according to the ancient mode of reckoning); three hours later, at 9 a.m., came Terce, then Sext just before noon, followed by Nones at 3 p.m.; Vespers was the evening office (around 5 p.m.), and Compline completed the day (around 6 p.m.). There was also one night service, Vigils, at 2 a.m. Benedict justified these eight daily prayers on the book of Psalms: "Seven times a day I praise thee," and "at midnight I rise to praise thee" (Psalm 119: 164 and 62).

It is hard to establish the precise times for these offices, especially since the monastic schedule was subject to variations conditioned by solar time and liturgical calendar. A brief summary of the year, as described in the Rule of Saint Benedict, however, is given below.

In winter (up till Easter), monks went to bed around 6:30 p.m., and began their day at 2 a.m. with Vigils, followed by study until it was time for Matins (between 3 and 5 a.m.). Matins was closely followed by Prime, which would end around 7 a.m. The day of manual labor and reading was then punctuated by the short offices of Terce, Sext and Nones (called "little hours"). After Nones the monks ate "dinner"—their first meal of the day—based on a menu of vegetables, wine, and a great deal of bread but never "the meat of four-footed animals" (RB 39: 11). They then read for two hours, before attending Vespers and Compline. This regimen was generally respected during the forty days of Lent, although the period of fasting was longer since the sole meal of the day was postponed until after Vespers, not before 6 p.m.

Summer began with Easter. The fifty days to Pentecost were a fortunate period with two meals a day (dinner at noon, supper after Vespers). From Pentecost to the Ides of September, the monks fasted two days per week—Wednesdays and Fridays—by having a single meal at Nones, thereby preparing themselves for the winter cycle. In summer they rose around 3 a.m. Shorter nights meant that Vigils had to be curtailed and followed immediately by Matins, resulting in two-and-a-half hours of service between 3 and 5 a.m. (RB 8). A restorative nap was therefore authorized between noon and 2 p.m. Manual work was done between Prime and Terce, reading between Terce and Sext. The monks dined at noon (except Wednesdays and Fridays following Pentecost, when the sole meal of the day would be taken after Nones), napped till 2 p.m., then worked until Vespers, and had supper, followed by Compline and bedtime around 7 or 8 p.m. The year was thus divided into two parts, summer (after Easter) and winter, but the start of winter was staggered depending on whether the modification involved meals (which changed on the Ides of September), the times of offices (which changed on November 1st), or sleep (naps eliminated on October 1st). The solar and liturgical years converged on Easter, which was never far from the vernal equinox (around March 25th). The forty days of Lent and the fifty days between Easter and Pentecost nevertheless constituted liturgical seasons unrelated to the stars. Furthermore, these solar and liturgical timetables were complicated by special cases. Saint Benedict had been sensitive to such cases, humanely leaving the monks some room to maneuver; the ill, the elderly, and the young, for example, received special dispensations in terms of the time and content of meals. Meanwhile, "hebdomadaries" (monks who took week-long turns performing the tasks of cooking or reading at mealtimes) were allowed to eat a light meal before they served the others (RB 35, 36, 37, 38). Often, the rule gives an abbot freedom to modify the precepts if necessary—which explains certain "irregularities" and the importance of customaries (or books of local custom) in knowing the actual daily life of each monastery.

The language of silence

Three chapters at the beginning of the Rule stress the virtues to be cultivated: obedience, silence, and humility (RB 5, 6, 7). It should be noted that "restraint of speech" comes in second place, before humility, not only as a mode of discipline but also as a virtue in itself. A monk was allowed to speak in the "council" (later called the chapter-house) in order to give his opinion (RB 3), to admit his faults, or to rebuke another monk in front of the community (RB 23). The rest of the time, silence was recommended, although mandatory only after Compline (RB 42), which suggests that it was not really total before then. Even during authorized times, monks were enjoined to "prefer moderation in speech and speak no foolish chatter, nothing just to provoke laughter; do not love immoderate or boisterous laughter" (RB 4: 53–55). In the refectory, only the reader should be heard, and

monks were instructed to ask for something "by an audible signal of some kind rather than by speech" (RB 38: 7) Ideally, the only good alternative to silence was the psalmody of divine services. Clearly then, use of the voice—for speech or song—was approved only when aimed at the entire community, for cenobitic ends. Conversely, mumbling and "grumbling" were corrupted modes of solitary expression, destined for no one but oneself (RB 5: 17 et *passim*).

Here again, over the centuries—and depending on the order—observance of silence could vacillate between Benedict's ideal and the leeway permitted by his Rule, not to mention uncorrected transgressions that slowly entered the customs of certain communities. Case-by-case studies being unfeasible here, just one highly surprising example will be mentioned: enjoined to maintain strict silence, monks at the Benedictine monastery of Hirsau in the Black Forest nevertheless communicated via a rich language of signs that enabled them to exchange all kinds of information, as reported in their customaries. Under the iron rule of Abbot William (1083–1088), entire chapters of customaries are devoted to a list of signs for nearly four hundred words, from signs for food (bread, indicated by a sign for baking), vegetables (distinguishing between beans, peas, lentils), even pots and pans, clothing, the times of services, etc. For example, to express Matins, a monk made the sign of the cross followed by the sign for sleep! The signs for buildings merit special attention: as with other terms in the vocabulary, an expression was conveyed in two stages—first a generic sign indicating a building (tipping straightened fingers together to create a roof) followed by the specific sign (for the church, a cross; for the chapter-house, beating the breast; for the parlor—called *auditorium*—a finger to the ear). Feigning sleep indicated the dormitory; eating, the refectory, shuddering with fever, the infirmary; sweltering, the warming room. To distinguish between kitchen and warm room, the sign for eating was added to that of heat. The library (*armarium*) was signified by holding a book. This little glossary of monastic life left no reality unstated—making the sign of a

CHAPTER-HOUSE, ALCOBAÇA (PORTUGAL).

REFECTORY, ALCOBAÇA (PORTUGAL).

building followed by clutching one's belly indicated the latrine! The cloister was defined by its function of circulation and distribution: making the roof-like sign for building, the index would then be pointed downward and turned in a circle. To make this circulation a sacred matter, a cross was first made with both index fingers, followed by the sign for moving around—thereby signifying a religious procession.

A time for everything

More than other buildings, the cloister was governed by alternating imperatives of speech and silence. Only silence was appropriate in the church, the dormitory, and the refectory (which resounded solely with collective psalmody or reading), whereas the parlor and the chapter-house were basically designed for speech. There remained the cloister, for which customaries were always careful to spell out the times of day and liturgical periods when monks had to remain silent. Of course, it should be pointed out that the Latin term *claustrum* might refer to the entire monastery as well as the architectural cloister, often playing on that metonymic confusion. At times when silence was imposed on the quadrangle of the cloister it was probably also imposed throughout the monastery. In contrast, however, it is clear that even when speech was permitted in the cloister, it was not allowed in the choir or refectory.

Information on the use of speech in cloisters can be gleaned from a look at several books of customs written between the tenth and twelfth centuries, notably Cluny's customaries and derivative documents as well as non-Cluniac texts from the abbeys of Fleury (France, tenth century), Eynsham (England, after 1004), and Fulda (Germany, eleventh century). Like requirements for fasting, silence in cloisters was governed by the liturgical season. Speaking there was forbidden on Mondays, Wednesdays, and Fridays during Lent, as well as during the Holy Week, and in the octave (eight-day period) following Easter and Pentecost. In contrast, talking was permitted every day until the Ides of September. Variations on these rules are too numerous to list here, but are related to specific days: during authorized summer days, for example, monks could talk immediately after the chapter-meeting that followed Prime, but on fast days only between Terce and Nones.

Permission to talk was almost always accompanied by an injunction to maintain discipline, specifically noting that all conversation must automatically end on the first stroke of canonical hours. Moderation in tone was required above all. "Hubbub in the cloister" was one of the twelve "bad habits in the cloister" listed by Hugo de Folieto in his mid twelfth-century *De claustro animae* (*Cloister of the Soul*, book II, chap. xi). Note how Hugo himself conflates the broader meaning of "cloister" with its physical meaning: among the *abusiones claustri* he first lists "the negligent priest, the disobedient disciple, the lazy young man, the stubborn old man, the fawning monk, the quibbling monk." Then he goes on to attack "costly dress and choice food," and finally enumerates the places where certain evils usually arise: "Noise in the cloister [*in claustro*], quarrels in the chapter-house, disunity in the choir, lack of respect at the altar." *Rumor in claustro*, the ninth of Hugo's twelve bad habits, was detailed in the twentieth chapter of his book. "Some [monks]. . . , when sitting in the cloister, do not attend to reading or silence, but rather to clamor and indiscretion. Never and nowhere respecting the time and place for speech and silence, they are always stirring pointlessly, calling out to all and sundry to converse with them." After having sketched this picture, Hugo comments on the principle of silence: "'Set a guard over my mouth, O Lord, keep watch over the door of my lips!' (Psalm 141: 3). The psalmist refers to a *door*, not to a wall. Had he said a wall, clearly permission to speak would be denied in all circumstances. But it is a door which, according to time and place, can open and close. There is a time and place for speech and for silence." Hugo's analysis then shifts slightly toward a distinction between appropriate use versus abuse of the voice. "This door opens at the time planned for reading, in the chapter-house for confession, in the church for prayer. And it closes in the cloister against gossip, in the chapter-house against poor

READER'S PULPIT IN REFECTORY, SANTA MARÍA HUERTA (SPAIN).   ENTRANCE TO CHAPTER-HOUSE, FONTFROIDE (FRANCE).

excuses, in the church against vain modulation of chant." Hugo concludes with the only type of clamor permitted: not tales of war between princes of the day (which monks liked to recount), but the completely internalized cry of the battle against temptation.

The rhythm of the seasons

More than other monastic buildings, the partly open cloister—overlooking nature in its little quadrangle—was subject to climatic variations. Vegetation provided the first evidence of seasonal change. "The green of the lawn in the middle of the physical cloister soothes the eyes of cloistered men and gives them more enthusiasm for reading," wrote Hugo de Folieto in another part of *De claustro animae* (III: xxxiv). Hugo's goal was to paint not a bucolic picture of the physical cloister but rather a moral picture of eternal virtues by contrasting the "variableness of time" with the "steadfastness of eternity." His vegetal metaphors served as counter-examples to demonstrate the fickleness of temporality. In the eternal cloister, he pointed out, the little garden "would neither grow in spring nor lose its vigor in autumn, would not become parched in the heat of summer nor benumbed in the cold of winter." Yet even taken negatively, this passage displays real sensitivity to the seasonal metamorphosis of colors in the cloister, and should not be overlooked if we wish to understand how cloisters functioned.

A few anecdotes record how violent storms could flood a cloister, or how ice and snow restricted access. A tenth-century English customary, the *Regularis Concordia*, reveals that the cloister was purely and simply abandoned during harsh English winters in favor of a closed, heated room where the entire community was allowed to gather on the express conditions of maintaining silence and not going there individually or on personal initiative (*Corpus consuetudinum monasticarum*—hereafter CCM—VII-3: 96, 1–6). In German lands, glazed cloisters appeared in the mid thirteenth century, the arcades being filled with panes of painted glass. Such cloisters flourished during the late Middle Ages.

THE COUNTLESS FUNCTIONS OF A CLOISTER

The expressions in Hirsau's sign language sum up a monastery's normal zones, yet indicate only a single activity for each one (the main one, admittedly). Elsewhere, however, records and customaries reveal the multiple functions of certain spaces. The cloister was undoubtedly the richest and most varied of all. It combined official functions with the most unofficial and domestic ones, making it a truly convivial space—in the sense of "living together"—within the cenobitic complex.

Spiritual breath

The cloister's primary function was to serve as a place for study and reading (both covered by the medieval Latin term *lectio*, making the distinction difficult). This function naturally required silence or, at the most, moderate and restrained speech. As the tenth-century *Regularis Concordia* put it, *tempus etiam lectionis est tempus taciturnitatis* (VII–3: 131, 20). Reading meant above all holy texts, oriented toward the Church fathers, biblical commentaries, and other kinds of exegetical or moral works. Monks were nevertheless allowed to read secular texts such as books on botany, poetry, music, and astrology, as mentioned at Cluny in 1252. Sacred reading, understood as *lectio divina*, was simply another type of prayer, which it nourished and reinforced, thereby clearly fulfilling the first of the two major objectives of Benedictine life. As the architectural lungs of the monastic system and the intellectual lungs of a monk's faith, the cloister enabled the monastery to breathe.

The organization of a monk's day comprised five or six hours of reading and study, roughly the same amount of time for work and canonical services, and an average of seven hours of sleep. Although never explicitly stated, reading probably took place partly in the church or even in the dormitory during winter, between Vigils and Matins, that is to say between 3:30 and 5:00 a.m., when the cold and dark were bitterest. Note, by the way, that in many monasteries, contrary to Saint Benedict's injunc-

MONT-SAINT-MICHEL (FRANCE).

SAINT-MARTIN-DU-CANIGOU (FRANCE).

tions, monks went back to sleep between these two services, and rested again between Matins and Prime, thereby altering their overall schedule. But once they had completely risen, it was customary after Prime (6:30 or 7 a.m.) for monks "to leave the church and sit in silence until Terce" (CCM VII-2: 248, 20–24). The rest of the day between Nones and Vespers was spent in the cloister, even in the darkest depths of winter when lights had to be set out (as testified by the fact that one of the tasks assigned to the "cellarer" was the refilling of such lamps). Unlike other rooms with small windows (often glazed with oiled paper), the cloister was the only place that benefited from fine lighting and natural sunshine. Monks either strolled slowly, book in hand, or stayed seated in the galleries on benches set along the wall. Seats were perhaps assigned. The principle that chatting could be prevented in the dormitory by interspersing the beds of the youngest brothers with those of the elder ones (RB 22: 7) was also apparently adopted for seating in the cloister. It was furthermore possible to take up a quill and write under the portico—in addition to the regular copying activity in the scriptorium—on the condition that the text was a *scriptura divina*.

Books came from the library, initially a simple *armarium* or cabinet set in one of the galleries, sometimes extending along the church wall, later becoming a separate room in monasteries where copying manuscripts became the monks' primary "manual labor," as indicated by inventories of their rich collections. According to the standards of the Rule, "during this time of Lent each [monk] is to receive a book from the library, and is to read the whole of it straight through" (RB 48: 15). A Cluniac customary from Wirzburg, dating from the eleventh century, suggests that a monk personally read only one book per year: the first Monday of Lent, "the librarian [*armarius*] shall bring the books to the chapter. . . [and] he shall read the list of books each brother had the preceding year. And when each one hears his name pronounced, he shall return his book and take another" (CCM VII-2: 294, 15–20). One book per year may have

been the minimum for certain zealous monks, yet such instructions inspire two comments: there must have been a rather mediocre level of intellectual or cultural ardor, and reading was probably done in a slow fashion based on repetition and rumination so that the book could be completely digested by the reader.

Schooling

The cloister was also a place for collective study as much as private reading. It is important to point out that a monastery included all age groups, from elderly monks to novices (both young and adult) to child oblates. Customaries use the Latin term *pueri*, or sometimes *infantes*, to refer both to young novices and to little children whose parents confided them to the monastery to be taught, fed (a not insignificant consideration for certain families), and ultimately turned into monks, whatever their religious calling. The tender age of these *pueri* becomes clearer when we recall that, in the thirteenth century, boys enrolled at university at the age of thirteen or fourteen. Often, *pueri* are mentioned only in the context of the dispensations they were granted from strict observance of the rule. Children sometimes lived according to a staggered schedule, as several Cluniac documents attest: there was a first signal that ended Matins for children, notifying their masters to take them back to the dormitory, whereas other monks had to wait for a subsequent signal (at Cluny, monks were allowed to go back to bed between early morning services, CCM VII-2: 73, 5). After mass, around Terce, children went to the refectory for a meal—even during Lent—while the brothers sat and read in the cloister; very little children were even allowed, after Prime, to have some bread and wine during school lessons (VII-2: 275, 14).

In the morning, children would attend classes from 7 a.m. until roughly 2:30 p.m., that is to say until Nones, with a pause for services and a snack around 10 a.m. After Prime, "once they have washed their hands, [the monks] shall sit to read or chant while children, at their lessons, shall read out loud, until the guardian gives the signal [for Terce and mass]"; or again, "they shall first begin to read out loud, then quietly they shall read or chant" (CCM VII-2: 275, 15). The students were then given a light meal. "On leaving the refectory, the children shall read again, in clear voices." Sext: "After Sext, they shall sit again and the children shall read most distinctly" (CCM VII-2: 394, 14). The cloister therefore literally served as a classroom for children, who were allowed and even encouraged to break the silence of the place in order to acquire learning. Sometimes, moreover, if a monk was disturbed and wanted to go into the church to continue reading silently, he was authorized to do so.

Perhaps a few school books, proverbs, or Aesop's fables enlivened the children's lessons, but since nothing is explicitly said about content, it was most certainly a psalter that was the key textbook. People learned to read from psalters—not just monks, but even King Louis IX of France in the early thirteenth century—in the same way that rabbinical schools used Leviticus to teach reading. Since monastic educational criteria evolved very little between the sixth and fourteenth centuries (as distinct from what occurred in lay schools), the psalter remained the sole reference work. A young brother would soon know it by heart from beginning to end, especially if he recited it out loud. All in all, a cloister fully broke its silence during school hours in order to ring louder and clearer with the verses of the psalms.

Psalmody and processions

Strikingly, all these records suggest that a monk's praying was done largely through reading, and that prayer and meditation without a written text were not mandatory exercises. Reading probably reduced the risk of yawning—or even falling asleep—after short nights. Customaries indicate that the main task of one monk called *circator* or *circa* (literally, "he who goes around") was to make sure that no one fell asleep during nocturnal offices (CCM VI-2: 273, 10). Instead of shaking the sloucher awake, the watchman set a lighted candle near him, probably to make his idleness clear to the others who could then rebuke him during chapter-house confessions.

Psalmody was halfway between reading and prayer, both personal expression without the hindrance of a book and an expression of orthodoxy deriving from a litany, antiphon, or response learned by heart. This above all meant the psalter, repeated from memory word for word—to the point that a monk was expected to confess in front of the chapter if he mangled a verse. After Prime on Good Friday, the Cluniac monks at Wirzburg would gather in the cloister and sing forty hymns from the psalter in their entirety, which apparently took them until Terce (CCM VII-2: 302, 3).

When chanting was not done seated, the community would do it while processing around the quadrangle. This might occur in the liturgical framework of Sundays, when all paraded in white robes, or during the Easter and Pentecost octaves (CCM VI-2: 385, 10). On Wednesdays and Fridays in winter and Lent, the procession was done barefoot. For certain ceremonies in addition to Sundays, such as the Purification of Mary, a cross was carried in front by the ministers, with candles and a sprinkling of holy water and incense (CCM VII-2: 342, 4). Palm Sunday was the occasion for the most significant procession, conducted in white garments and incorporating not only the blessing of the palms (CCM VII-2: 62, 25), but also a station before the door of every monastic building, which the priest blessed by invoking Christ's entry into Jerusalem (CCM VII-2: 400, 10).

Physical hygiene

Cloisters endowed with a fountain or pool, as was always the case with Cistercian abbeys, boasted a plumbing system that made access to clean water easy. That is why the cloister became the authorized site of various ablutions, from washing the hands to washing clothes. Monks had to wash after the service of Prime (in customaries which allowed the monks to go back to sleep between Matins and Prime, they could arrive for prayer in bedsocks). The cook and sacristan would leave the service before the final psalms in order to get shod and washed first. Once Prime was over, it was the turn of the other monks. A special corner of the cloister was specially reserved for brushing one's hair, although we do not know which one or why (CCM VII-2: 275, 15). The monks were obliged to pass through the cloister to reach the refectory, and therefore were also obliged to wash hands and feet before the meal. Nearby were a selection of towels for drying themselves, which the cooks were expressly forbidden to use as dishtowels or other linen. Washing the feet was both a hygienic necessity and a symbolic ritual. The Rule of Saint Benedict specifies that the monk on weekly kitchen duty will complete his turn on Sunday, and that "on Saturday the brother who is completing his work will do the washing. He is to wash the towels which the brothers use to wipe their hands and feet. Both the one who is ending his service and the one who is about to begin are to wash the feet of everyone" (RB 35: 7–9). It is obvious that this operation reflects an ideal of humil-

LAVABO, SANTA CRUZ DE COIMBRA (PORTUGAL).

WELL, MONTMAJOUR (FRANCE).

ity and service modeled on Christ's washing of the disciples' feet just before the Last Supper.

The cloister was also the stage for communal shaving. Shaving and bathing were a ritual obligation fives times per year: after Prime on Holy Saturday (it is worth noting that on Good Friday the brothers went barefoot part of the day in penitence, see CCM VII-2: 263, 12), on Pentecost, Christmas, All Saints' Day, and the feast day of the local saint. The rest of the time, bathing was generally discouraged, except for the ill. Nor was bathing done in the cloister, apparently. In contrast, the shaving of beards and tonsures was more frequent, once every three weeks or so. This was more than a question of cleanliness, for it reasserted a monk's distinctive features (clean-shaven and tonsured) and also reinforced the principle of mutual aid. The monks sat in two lines, facing each other, in one of the galleries of the cloister, so that while one group used the razor, the other held the basin—then they swapped roles. If the Cluniac customaries are to be believed, shaving was a fully cenobitic act.

Laundry

The brothers' hand towels were washed once a week. The operation was probably straightforward compared to the periodic washing of clothes. According to Benedict, "to provide for laundering and night wear, every monk will need two cowls and two tunics, but anything more must be taken away as superfluous" (RB 55: 10–11). The frequency of this laundering is not specified in the chronicles, and since Benedictine rule authorized several dispensations concerning the number of monastic garments, on laundry day the cloister must have been transformed into one big soapy dispensary, with tunics on one side, stockings or underwear on another, and bedsocks of every size everywhere! Better still, clotheslines were run along the galleries where this entire wardrobe was hung to dry. Only the gallery with the

chapter-house (and parlor) was spared, because of all the coming and going. When everything was dry, the clothes were folded and set on benches in the cloister, each monk having to recognize and claim his own habit. Here again a *circator* was charged with overseeing the operation: "After Compline, he shall make a tour of the cloister and if he finds a book or garment, he will bring it to the chapter-house the next day"—where the forgetful monk would obviously have to make a public confession (CCM VII-3: 132, 14).

The airing of dormitory mattresses, as reported in an eleventh-century customary from Fulda/Trier, probably took place in the cloister. Between the chapter meeting and Sext on Good Friday and the feast day of the local saint, it was expected that "all will carry together, on that day, their bedding and beat it in the heat of the sun." After Sext, "once again, when the straw on the bed has been changed, all will taking their bedding back and prepare their beds, until the first stroke of the hour of Nones" (VII-3, 300: 3-7). The ground of the cloister itself was strewn with rushes, which the cellarer was expected to change periodically.

Finally, other functional aspects of a cloister are worth mentioning: from one of the columns would hang a sharpening stone for knives, which monks were allowed to use at times when talking was permitted. Copyists in the scriptorium could also go sharpen their nibs there. Only the chamberlain, who looked after the razors, was allowed to use the sharpening stone during periods of silence, and only on condition that the reading of the other monks was not disturbed.

FOUNTAIN, JÉRONIMOS, BELÉM (PORTUGAL).

FOUNTAIN, SANTA CRUZ DE COIMBRA (PORTUGAL).

URBAN CLOISTERS

The architectural form of cloisters remained generally unchanged down through the centuries. And yet distinctions emerge once we examine the architecture in terms of function and use rather than form. There were cloisters for monks (at monasteries), cloisters for canons regular (at cathedrals and collegiate churches), and cloisters for mendicant friars. All cloisters may have looked similar, but they harbored different modes of religious life. Often, cloisters can be immediately classified according to location—some are lost in the wilderness, others are set in the center of towns. This general feature should not be applied too systematically, however, because on occasion Benedictine priories were founded in towns, while a village may have grown up around a formerly isolated monastery; canon priests, meanwhile, may have been attached to suburban or rural churches, indeed to a church at the foot of some lordly château outside the village. So it is important to know in each case for whom the cloister was built; depending on whether it was intended for monks, canons, or mendicant friars, a cloister would not serve the same purpose despite similar appearance.

The institution of canons

In the Carolingian meaning of the term, a canon was a cleric who had acceded to the major orders and was therefore a priest (or, exceptionally, a deacon), and who lived with other priests alongside a large church. Together, these priests formed a chapter of canons, specified as a cathedral chapter when it was attached to a bishop's church (cathedral). At the time of the Carolingian reforms, these canons were obliged to adopt a communal lifestyle, in some respects quite similar to the cenobitic life of monks. The regulations, known as the Rule of Aachen, were issued during a synod at Aachen in 816, one year before it was decided to unify all monasteries under the Benedictine rule. Both measures reflected the same goal. Aachen's canonical rule was partly based, for that matter, on the Benedictine-like and almost monastic tone of the system imposed sixty years earlier, around 755, by the Frankish bishop Chrodegang on the clergy at Metz, over whom he exercised episcopal authority. Canons had to worship during the divine offices, eat and sleep in a community, remain chaste, and live in an enclosure (*claustrum*). Major differences with monasticism remained, however: since a canon had taken no vow of poverty, he could receive the income from his own property or that of the community (houses, lands, fees for saying masses) in the form of a stipend known as a prebend. Life was also less ascetic (canons could notably eat meat), and much more time was devoted to offering hospitality and performing works of mercy and charity in local society (chapter 145 of the Aachen Rule instructs canons to "hearten the poor, dress the naked, visit the ill, bury the dead, console the afflicted"). Canons therefore had permission to leave the cloister, even though their primarily role was not to serve the parish, which was the job of other clergy (whom the bishop or chapter had not chosen as canons). For women, there existed religious institutions designed along similar lines, which granted "canonesses" broad freedom to go out and maintain regular contact with their families and the outside world; such establishments were often called abbeys, but might be considered boarding schools for daughters of the nobility, especially within the Holy Roman Empire.

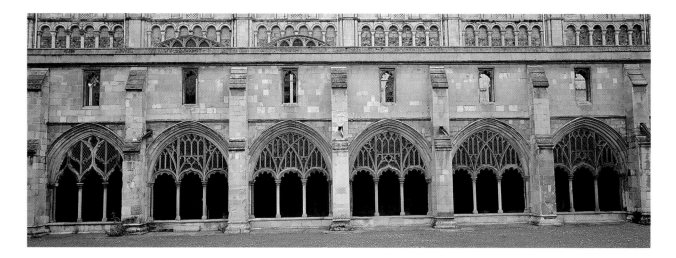

NORWICH (ENGLAND).

Canons regular, canons secular

The *Institutio canonicorum* of 816 accorded a dispensation to certain canons who were old or ill, allowing them to have a private little house within the canonical enclosure, thereby not having to sleep in the dormitory. What was originally a special concession soon became a general practice—canons abandoned dormitory and refectory for small individual dwellings within the cloistered enclosure, which might be fairly extensive, becoming an entire canonical neighborhood. The college of canons was soon gathering solely for daily services and for meetings to manage collective property. The original Carolingian institution was further sabotaged by the social disturbances of the late tenth century and eleventh century, combined with the appropriation of ecclesiastical machinery by temporal lords (which also disrupted monastic reform). The significant appeal of the prebend (which meant that canons were almost exclusively recruited from the ranks of the nobility), plus numerous incidents of concubinage and the abandonment of all parish service, spurred occasional attempts at reform starting in the year 1000. Rome then tried to establish some control in the eleventh century through the Gregorian reform movement.

The eleventh century was a great century for reforms: not only monastic reform under the aegis of the abbots at Cluny, but also papal and ecclesiastical reform under the impetus of the popes, notably Gregory VII (1073–1085) after whom it was named. This development continued throughout the twelfth century. The popes' efforts at reform consisted of liberating the clergy from lay society in order to distinguish better the spiritual from the temporal, with the ultimate goal of giving priority to the spiritual. Papal decrees condemned simony (the selling of sacraments) and Nicolaitism (priests who lived in a conjugal relationship). And what better way to separate the clergy from lay society than to advocate the monastic ideal? That meant insisting on vows of poverty, imposing celibacy and chastity. As far as canons were concerned, a Lateran Council decision of 1059 urged them to return to a truly communal lifestyle (implying chastity) and above all to renounce personal property. Such renunciation did not mean the community abandoned its wealth, but wealth was to be shared among all members. Reaction to these council recommendations varied greatly depending on the ecclesiastical region. In northern France and the Rhineland, most cathedral chapters clung to the Aachen rule, refusing to renounce their prebends or abandon their organizational independence (which might vary from one diocese to another according to local tradition). In southern France and Italy, on the other hand, the reform was adopted more widely. There thus emerged, in the mid eleventh century, a distinction between "canons regular" and "canons secular." The distinction remained significant until the fourteenth century when the regular communities, scattered into small groups that were financially and jurisdictionally isolated, went into decline. They were gradually secularized, restoring personal property to each member, who managed it individually.

The Augustinian Rule

Canons regular of the eleventh century were no longer satisfied with the Aachen Rule, which was left to canons secular in its lax form. They thus turned to a document called the Rule of Saint Augustine. In fact, Augustine of Hippo was a Doctor of the Church who never drew up a rule in the strict sense of the term; but as priest and bishop he was led to approve the rule of a monastery in Tagaste, to issue instructions for a monastery in his home town of Hippo, and to write a letter of reproach to nuns who had rebelled against their prioress. His "rule" was therefore compiled from a series of texts that circulated in various or abridged forms. Reformed canons of the eleventh and twelfth centuries primarily followed the relatively flexible precepts called the *regula prima*, which called for obedience, worship at the offices, communal mass, abstinence, simplicity in dress, and above all renunciation of personal property. "Call nothing your own, but let everything be yours in common" (Rule of Augustine, 1:3). The model invoked by Augustine was that of the early community of Jerusalem described in the Acts of the Apostles (4: 32–35)—"everything was shared by the earliest Christians, and distributed to each according to his needs." The canonical lifestyle, then, like the monastic one, was based on the idea of a return to apostolic life. But even though similarities linked priestly monks in the abbeys to monkish priests in the reformed canonical churches, their statuses remained fundamentally distinct. A canon was above all a member of the clergy and could be assigned to a parish church and the *cura animorum* (cure of souls), even if that occurred fairly rarely. A canon focused on preaching and the speculative studies that went with it.

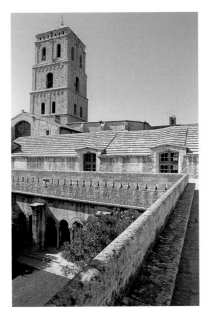

SAINT-TROPHIME, ARLES (FRANCE).

The canonical "monastery" of Saint-Victor in Paris, for instance, was famous for the influence of its doctrinal school, thanks to canons such as Hugues (died 1141) and Richard (died 1173). Every chapter therefore had its own personality; the world of canons regular was generally as varied—depending on the aspiration of local chapter and diocese—as that of canons secular.

The mendicant orders

Only now is it necessary to discuss the mendicant orders, which were highly active in urban settings. They include the Minors and Preachers, and—discussed more briefly—the Carmelites and Augustinians, who form the four mendicant families. Chronology supports this timing, since the orders were founded during the thirteenth century, yet it is their specific status that truly dictates it, since they resembled the reformed canonical order in certain aspects. The original mendicants were not monks, for instance, even though they lived in monasteries. How could they be monks, for that matter? Their only sustenance came from begging—the good will of the faithful—or from the sweat of their brows, rather than from the income of the community's property. The founder of the Friars Minor (or Franciscans) was an Italian saint, Francis of Assisi (c. 1182–1226), while the crucial figure for the Preachers (or Dominicans) was a Castilian saint, Dominic of Calaruega (c. 1170–1221). Mendicants went into the world, settling at the edge or even in the center of towns. A well-known saying summed up the difference between the various callings: *Bernadus valles, montes Benedictus amabat, oppida Franciscus, celebres Dominicus urbes* (Bernard liked valleys, Benedict the mountains, Francis market-towns, Dominic populous cities). The Franciscans, like the Preachers, soon abandoned market-towns for the suburbs and cities, because the lay population was their raison d'être, given their calling as preachers and pastors.

In 1215, it should be recalled, the Fourth Lateran Council forbade the establishment of new forms of religious order. Thus, in 1216, Dominic simply adopted the Rule of Saint Augustine so that his Order of Preachers could be ratified, although perhaps more from choice than obligation, since he himself belonged to the canonical tradition. In contrast, the Friars Minor, claiming that Innocent III had orally authorized Francis's early fraternity back in 1209, were able to negotiate a rule specific to their institution in 1223.

Canonical cloisters

Cenobitic and communal habits were crucial aspects of the monastic rule; breaking them meant destroying the identity of the cenobitic monk. For canons, however, communal life was periodically interrupted by the cure of souls outside the enclosure, and by care for the lay population. Did the "continuous communality" of monks and the "discontinuous communality" of canons therefore represent two lifestyles, implying two categories of cloister? Was the cloister as crucial to canonical existence as it was to monastic life? Before attempting a reply, a few comments are in order. Specialists in canonical architecture regret the paucity of information available on canonical cloisters and customs. The limited nature of excavations (often difficult to perform in urban environments) and the ambiguity of written documents (*claustrum* and *claustra* meaning either cloister or the entire enclosure) do not always allow us to assert the existence of an architectural cloister before the eleventh and especially the twelfth century. The cathedral of Saint-Nazaire in Autun in northern France, for example, must have had its own cloister by the end of the ninth century, whereas we cannot be certain that cloisters were adopted in the south of France before 1100. Furthermore, subsequent destruction has scrambled important analytical information; thus in France, an impressive number of canonical enclosures vanished during the French Revolution, and it is no longer possible to reconstruct accurately their Romanesque or Gothic cloisters, nor the buildings that flanked the main diocesan churches.

In order to study canonical cloisters, it is necessary to refine once again the distinction between canons regular and canons secular, between the intense if discontinuous communality of the regulars and the minimized, sometimes even occasional, communality of the seculars. In a regular chapter, communal spaces were identical to those used by monks: dormitory, refectory, chapter-house, and perhaps the storehouses. The cloister was almost always designed to extend along four sides, retaining its function as point of transit from one building to another. Yet the overall arrangement of the communal buildings was subject to many variations, depending on the landscape and the degree of communality of the canonical chapter. These variations, unlike the uniformity of the Benedictine model, prevented the rise of a systematic pattern for canonical cloisters.

Examples are even more varied when it comes to cloisters for the secular canonry. Many were cathedral cloisters, which flourished between the twelfth and sixteenth centuries. In canonical quarters where each

BATALHA (PORTUGAL).

canon had his own house, there was no longer any reason for a dormitory, which vanished. The communal partaking of meals was also slowly abandoned, although the refectory was retained as a room to be used for certain celebrations and ceremonies—that was where the daily bread and wine bestowed on resident canons were distributed. The chapter-house therefore became the key canonical space. In theory, a chapter meeting was held there every day (maintained by the regulars until their secularization in the late Middle Ages), usually after Prime, like monks, and involving a sermon, prayer, reading, and confession of sins. In practice, however, the chapter-house was used above all for general meetings of the canonry, designed to settle spiritual, material, and political matters.

Appearance or reality?

For canons secular, there was clearly a discrepancy between a cloister's architectural layout and its use. The cloister was drained, so to speak, of its meaning in the full sense of its cenobitic role. The quadrangular arrangement of galleries designed as living space was now just a meaningless echo of a collective aspiration, a hollow symbol of communality—indeed, an alibi. Cloisters for canons, especially when built next to a cathedral, betrayed an aesthetics of power, as did the bishop's church. By the twelfth century, then, secular cloisters were providing a demonstration of the glamour of the "Benedictine pattern" and its widespread imitation as an architectural model.

But what of regular chapters? In the south of France, it would appear that canons regular only built their physical cloister several decades after having adhered to the Augustinian Rule, from the mid twelfth century or so, that is to say a fairly long time after their adoption of the Gregorian reform. The only counter-example to this general trend was Arles, where the late adoption of the rule was accompanied by the immediate construction of a cloister from 1180 onward. Elsewhere, the cloister was not considered an indispensable condition

<small>CATHEDRAL CLOISTER, LEÓN (SPAIN).</small>

of communal life; at first, the canons were content with a "common house" which contained all the necessary rooms in a single building. It might be concluded that their cloister, like that of canons secular, was just a sign of architectural ostentation, a simple imitation of a monastic motif. And yet it should be recalled that, unlike Carolingian monastic reform, the Gregorian reform merely encouraged rather than imposed the regularization of canons. Canonical flexibility should therefore not be compared with monastic uniformity. Furthermore, money being the main problem for the new order of regulars, financial questions were perhaps the reason for avoiding such expense at an early stage. Finally, the increasing identification of monks with the priesthood, largely used by the Gregorians clearly to distinguish clergy from laity, seems not to have truly made an impression until the twelfth century. The treatise by canon Hugo de Folieto, *De claustro animae*, imposing a veritable monastic ideal on canons regular, was only written in the 1130s. In my opinion, this makes it impossible to view all canonical cloisters with the same eye and, in the case of cloisters for the regular canonry, invalidates the argument of artifice or ostentation.

The existence of a cloister was therefore not determined by the regularity or secularity of canons. And yet its use, spiritual ramifications, and above all the organization of surrounding buildings depended crucially on that distinction. In the canonical world, unlike its monastic twin, there was no single, inviolable pattern for cloisters.

Mendicant cloisters

When Dame Poverty asked to see their cloister, the Friars Minor climbed to the top of a hill and pointed to the world that lay at their feet. That quaint allegorical tale, recounted in a Franciscan treatise from the 1240s, reflects the Minors' ideals of a wandering life of preaching, of staying in contact with nature—a thousand leagues from monastic principles. Yet this vision was already utopian by the mid thirteenth century because the Franciscans could not escape the influence of the monastic model right from the drafting of its rule in 1223, eventually abandoning the term "brotherhood" for "order," establishing institutional structures, and even building permanent monasteries to accompany the exponential success of the movement. However, due either to construction costs or wariness, the Franciscans avoided building four-sided cloisters until the middle of the fourteenth century.

On the other hand, the affiliation of the Dominicans with canons regular made their use of a cloister more natural. A passage in Jacobus de Voragine's *Golden Legend* (written circa 1265) alludes to a cloister-like space when recounting Dominic's encounter with the devil in a monastery in Bologna. Praying in the church at night, Dominic motioned to a brother who was prompting him to go to bed (note the respect for silence after Compline, which meant communicating in sign language). The saint then recognized the devil's face underneath the cowl and forced him to confess how he tempted the other brothers, dragging him from place to place. In the choir, the devil admitted, "I make them come too late and leave too soon!" In the dormitory, he said, "I make them sleep too long and rise late so that they miss the office, and I give them impure thoughts." In the refectory, the demon confessed, "I tempt some of the brothers to eat too much, and so they sin by gluttony, and others I tempt to eat too little and so they become weak in the service of God and the observance of the rule." In the parlor, the devil felt at home: "This place belongs entirely to me! When the friars come here to talk, I studiously tempt them to prattle all at the same time, to confuse each other with idle words, and never to wait to hear what the other is saying." But when Dominic led him to the chapter-house, the alarmed devil would not go in, saying, "Here [the brothers] confess . . . here they are absolved! And so, to my chagrin, I lose all I had been so happy to win elsewhere!"

This fable takes readers through a monastic-type enclosure. Starting in the thirteenth century, a few large Dominican monasteries in Italy (Santa Sabina in Rome and Santa Maria Novella in Florence) returned to the standard pattern of a cloister with four galleries. It should not be forgotten, however, that the cityscape and cost of urban land meant that both Franciscan and Dominican monasteries often had just a single communal building that left no room for a cloister. Moreover, a cloister is not mentioned explicitly in the account by Jacobus, either as a space for walking or as a place of temptation.

The mendicants did not have a unique attitude toward cloisters—either they did without one completely or they opted for a glamorous model. This suggests a comparison with canons: in the former case, the mendicants acted like canons regular in the early days; in the latter, conversely, their superb cloisters were similar to the ostentatious architecture of cathedral chapters. We can only deduce that by the late Middle Ages a non-monastic cloister conveyed an image of power; its absence represented willful poverty. It neither case, however, was it any longer the key feature of communal life.

The uses of urban cloisters

The multifarious religious lifestyles in cities, whether canonical or mendicant, explain the disparity and variety of functions of urban cloisters. For canons regular, they apparently played a role similar to the one performed in monasteries: a space for reading and study, for giving lessons to children and sometimes all canons, climate permitting. The presence of many stone benches can be noted even if, in southern France, no place for the traditional *armarium* was provided. Also in the monastic tradition, urban cloisters—depending on the community—often maintained the liturgical value of the space: galleries were used for processions on Sundays or other celebrations, as indicated by customaries and canonical statutes. In the regular chapter of Maguelone, for example, the daily office of Vespers was celebrated there. In particular, the ritual washing of the feet took place there on Maundy Thursday and Holy Saturday (if sometimes moved to the refectory). On such occasions, the ritual water was probably drawn from the adjacent well. Apart from that, it does not appear that canonical cloisters were used for public washing or laundry sessions—as was the case in monasteries—which the existence of individual houses rendered unnecessary.

So what special uses of canonical cloisters distinguished them from monastic ones? Canons willingly used the cloister as a burial place, which monks rarely did, reserving that honor almost solely for their abbots. Tombs proliferated in canonical galleries; as excavations at Viviers show, up to the late thirteenth century not only canons and other clergy were buried there, but also laymen, children, and even a few women.

Urban cloisters owed their specificity to contact with the world. The school might accept young clergy from outside the diocese, which led to the international fame of certain cathedral schools until they were dethroned by universities during the age of scholasticism. The poor could enter the cloister for the distribution of alms or food, which might also be done in the refectory (at Auch from 1175 onward, at Lyon and Arles in the thirteenth century). In Tournai, for example, townspeople met in the cloister at certain times to settle public matters. Here and there, cloisters apparently served as little more than a godsend for merchants who used the covered galleries to protect their goods—at Angers in 1093, spices were sold there and money-changers even set up their tables. The legal immunity enjoyed by the canonical enclosure was obviously not alien to its mercantile, bourgeois appeal. In short, even as the cloister opened onto the city and its affairs, the city brought some of its customs and values into the cloister.

BENCHES AND TOMBS, SANTES CREUS (SPAIN).

THE BEAUTY OF CLOISTERS

METAPHORICAL ARCHITECTURE

The spiritual cloister

Medieval Christian rhetoric, derived as it was from ancient allegory, evangelical parable, and exegetical commentary, liked to reveal a spiritual meaning behind the literal meaning of every text, even if that meant artificially generating one. This spiritual meaning might be typological (or allegorical), moral, or anagogical. A typological interpretation revealed how an incident from the Old Testament prefigured one in the New, a moral one yielded useful lessons in life, and an anagogical one uncovered the eschatological promise of an afterlife. As a thirteenth-century Latin saying put it, "the letter teaches what happened, allegory what is to be believed, morality what should be done, anagogy what is to be hoped."

Cloisters were viewed as a text to be read spiritually. Right from the ninth century, the plan of Saint Gall was invested with a symbolic meaning alongside its functional purpose. The Latin captions labeling each building also gave detailed figures—the width of the main nave of the abbey church was forty feet, the width of the transepts were twenty feet, and the overall length was 200 feet. The figure forty therefore served as the basic module of construction, since all dimensions were multiples of forty. The cloister, meanwhile, was laid out in a perfect square 100 by 100 feet. Special symbolism lies behind this modular geometry. According to biblical tradition, forty is the figure associated with events calling for attitudes cultivated by monks, namely patience and penitence: for forty days, the flood covered the world and buffeted Noah's ark; the people of Israel had to wander in the desert for forty years before reaching the promised land; forty days was the time spent by Moses on Mount Sinai before receiving the tablets with the

NOIRLAC (FRANCE).

Law, and was also the deadline that Jonah gave to Nineveh to avoid destruction, and the period that the resurrected Christ spent with his disciples between Easter and Ascension.

The four sides of the courtyard triggered additional allusions: the four elements and the four seasons suggested that the cloister was a miniature world; the four rivers of paradise and the four cardinal virtues made it a moral world, too; the four great prophets, the four evangelists, and the four letters of the Hebrew name for God (YHVH, or Yahweh) pointed to the cloister as another holy tetrad.

In the twelfth century, Hugo de Folieto composed *De claustro animae*, his treatise on the "cloister of the soul," along architectural lines. In book III, he persistently pursues the metaphor of cloister and soul, playing on the multiple meanings of the term cloister (which sometimes refers to the entire monastery, sometimes just the quadrangle). "The cloister of the soul is named contemplation. Because within the bosom [of contemplation], while the mind ponders, the soul alone meditates on heaven, cutting itself off from earthly things and remaining aloof from the agitation of thoughts of the flesh." The physical cloister is central to Hugo's symbolic monastery. "The perimeter of the cloister is adorned with columns of virtue, it is supported by bases of patience, its square is perfected by the rule of justice, it is fortified by the dwellings near the virtues, and a wall of good deeds surrounds the outside of the cloister which, by keeping the door of silence closed, prevents wandering minds from getting in" (chap. i). The rest of the description is organized around the regular plan of the building, which includes the soul's chapter-house (a passage on confession), the soul's refectory (spiritual nourishment), the soul's dormitory (inner peace), and the soul's oratory (prayer).

Just as the *claustrum materiale* lends its form to the *claustrum morale*, so the moral cloister imbues the material cloister with a heavy symbolic charge in return. The four sides of the square assume a religious nature: the west wing represents disregard for oneself; the north wing, disregard for the world; the east, love of God; the south, love of one's neighbor (chap. ii). The columns that have been cut, sculpted, and worn smooth are seen as encouragement to cut oneself from vice, to turn one's hand to spiritual projects, to bear the tribulations of adversity. Twelve types of column are identified, representing as many virtues: "humility of heart, affliction of flesh, softness of conversation, coarseness of clothing, moderation in food, seriousness in work, love of submission, contempt for honors, flight from praise, acceptance of others' opinions, deference to subordinates, mistrust of self" (chap. iii). The alloys used for the bases of columns become moral emblems: bronze for courage, silver for clarity, gold for dazzling illumination. "Courage in action, clarity in conversation, illumination of intelligence. Whoever displays endurance under these three forms can bear with firmness, like a base of gold, the masonry of virtues" (chap. iv). Moralized and personified by Hugo, a cloister becomes a model of virtue and meditation, as eloquent in stone as a treatise on spirituality.

Prison or paradise?

In the twelfth and thirteenth centuries, any defense and illustration of cloistered life would exploit the ambivalent nature of enclosure. Insofar as its inhabitants could not leave the enclosure, a cloister was like a prison (active enclosure), but since no aggression from the outside world could enter, it was also a haven (passive enclosure), indeed a kind of paradise. The monk Honorius Augustodunensis (died 1157) evoked the various meanings of "cloistered life" under ten headings in a brief treatise, *De vita claustrali*. Honorius described a cloister via metaphors both salutary and severe: a shore sheltered from the storm, beneficial shade from the sun, a restful bed for weary laborers, a refuge for fugitives and the guilty, a school for infants taught by Christ, a training ground for battle against vice, a prison where criminals learn to merit heaven, a path of temptation, an inferno where penitents atone but the hard-hearted are crucified; a paradise where everyone can feast on Scripture. These comparisons underwent further amplification in *De disciplina claustrali*, composed several decades later by Peter of Celle (died 1183), the famous abbot of Saint-Remi in Reims who became bishop of Chartres. According to Peter, the cloister was by turns a substitute for the cross, a stadium, a treasure house, a royal bedchamber, a torture rack. Living there meant being saved in the ark with Noah, surviving in the belly of a whale with Jonah, being consecrated in the maternal womb with Jeremiah, seeking the desert with John the Baptist, hearing the angelic greeting with Mary, sitting before the doctors of the temple with Jesus, awaiting the descent of the Holy Ghost with the apostles (chap. vii). An acolyte of cloistered discipline was compared to the young Esther in the Old Testament, down to the nuptial metaphor: chosen with other virgins throughout the kingdom to pleasure the king, Esther awaited his call by anointing herself with oil of myrtle and other precious ointments, until the moment when the king summoned her for the night; "likewise the great King, the King of kings, summons those He has chosen, assembling all in the discipline of the cloister. . . on the day appointed from all eternity, he will have them come to the nuptial bed in the chamber of glory and the blessed life" (chap. iv).

There were endless variants on the theme of the clois-

ter. Here it might be described as the antechamber—sometimes pleasant, sometimes painful—to an audience with God. "Those who bear troubles and trials of the worldly cloister for a time, will live near angels in endless peace in that cloister not fashioned by human hands [i.e., heaven]," wrote Hugo de Folieto in book IV of *De claustro animae*, superimposing heaven and cloister in one of his finest analogies. Elsewhere, the cloister might be an earthly doublet of the paradise lost by our Edenic ancestors (or an anticipation of the heavenly one to come). At even greater length than *De vita claustrali*, Honorius Augustodunensis returned to this metaphor in *Gemma animae* (Ornament of the Soul): "The cloister represents paradise, the monastery [represents] the garden of Eden, the most peaceful place in paradise. Its fountain of sensuality becomes the baptismal font in the monastery; the tree of life in Eden is the body of our Lord in the monastery. The various fruit trees are the various books of Holy Scripture. The solitude of the cloister presents the image of heaven: in the same way as heaven separates the just from sinners, so the cloister separates disciples of a religious life from worldly men. Even more, the monastery represents heavenly paradise: the fountain and tree of life designate Christ, who is the fountain of life and the nourishment of the blessed who live for eternity. In the monastery, two choirs sing the praise of God together; and in heavenly paradise, the angels and saints will praise in sweet concert for all eternity." This last phrase is an allusion to the choir of the lay brothers, adopted by almost every monastery. It is clear that Honorius is employing a monastic model as opposed to a canonical one. Alluding to John 14:2 ("In my Father's house are many rooms"), he concludes, "In the cloister, everyone has his place according to his rank, just as in paradise everyone receives a room according to his merits."

"If I forget you, O Jerusalem"

Among the various names commonly adopted for the cloister in religious literature, "the portico of Solomon" in Jerusalem combined an architectural analogy with a spiritual goal. This image was used allusively by Hugo in *De claustro animae*, then more clearly by Honorius in *Gemma animae*, and again by Sicard (ordained bishop of Cremon in 1185) in his *Mitrale*, and once again by William Durandus (bishop of Mende in 1286) in his *Rationale divinorum officiorum* (Manual of Divine Offices). These images are summed up by a passage in Honorius: "The edifice of the cloister alongside the monastery was taken from the portico of Solomon alongside the Temple. There, all the disciples lived together as one soul." For Sicard and William Durandus, the portico thus corresponded to "the place where the Levites watched and slept," the members of the tribe of Levi being the priests of Israel (*Rationale*, I: xliii).

Fundamental concepts of cenobitic life converge here. To explain their lifestyle, monks referred to two illustrious models from the New Testament: the company of apostles who gathered in one place on the day of Pentecost (Acts 2:1), and the first Christian community of Jerusalem (Acts 4:32). The Temple of Jerusalem, with its many courtyards and four covered galleries, was the temple par excellence. That was where Christ taught, a temple that He compared to Himself by offering to "raise it up again" in three days (John 2: 19); it was therefore a temple of stone that afforded priceless allusions, both historical and moral. By Jesus's day, Solomon's temple had been replaced by Herod's, but the east gallery was still called "the portico of Solomon," linking it to the most holy antiquity. A symbolic connection to the apostles was further encouraged by a passage in John that describes Jesus coming and going under this portico (John 10: 23), although nowhere, to my knowledge, was it expressly stated that the apostles actually lived there.

The theme of apostolic life as adopted by monks also became a model for canons during the Gregorian reform, one crucial difference being that canons were open to the lay world (like the missionary apostles after Pentecost), whereas monks above all followed the apostolic example of abandoning personal property and living communally. Canons regular led a simultaneously communal and apostolic life through preaching, hospitality, and the cure of souls. From the Gregorian standpoint, such clergymen therefore followed the *vita vere apostolica* (true apostolic life) in all its richness. Thus the phrase "portico of Solomon," once extended to cover the priestly Levites, could flow from the pens of Sicard (who had been a canon in Mainz) and William Durandus (a former papal cleric). Historical Jerusalem, earthly Jerusalem, and heavenly Jerusalem: all these mysterious, sacred concepts resonated in the alert ear of a monk or canon meditating in the arcade of a cloister.

THE SPIRIT OF DECORATION

Historiated versus aniconic cloisters

The spiritual literature on cloisters discussed above did

not address the issue of decorating the architectural ensemble. The only references, from a moral and symbolic perspective, were to the principles of a quadrilateral, of columns supporting the roof, and of bases of various materials—all of which basically evoke geometric, abstract shapes. Yet a famous letter by Saint Bernard shows that decoration was a spiritual issue within the cloister. Written around 1123, this *Apologia* was addressed to William, the Benedictine abbot of Saint-Thierry (in the archdiocese of Reims), who became the friend and biographer of Saint Bernard. After having criticized the lavishness of churches, Bernard attacked cloisters: "What profit is there in those ridiculous monsters, in that marvelous and deformed beauty, in that beautiful deformity? To what purpose are those unclean apes, those fierce lions, those monstrous centaurs, those half-men, those striped tigers, those fighting knights, those hunters winding their horns? Many bodies are there seen under one head, or again, many heads to a single body. Here is a four-footed beast with a serpent's tail; there, a fish with a beast's head. Here again the forepart of a horse trails half a goat behind it, or a horned beast bears the hind-quarters of a horse. In short, so many and so marvelous are the varieties of shapes on every hand, that we are more tempted to read in the marble than in our books, and to spend the whole day wondering at these things rather than in meditating the law of God."

Bernard's pen makes the varied, fantastic creatures haunting Romanesque cloisters spring to life before our very eyes. The abbot of Clairvaux might have seen such carved motifs at Cluny or another Cluniac priory, but he was not specific in his criticisms, aiming them at all Benedictine monasteries, not just Cluny. Under Bernard's direct influence, the Cistercians would ultimately renounce all decorative ornamentation not only in the church but in the rest of the abbey. The stylistic history of Cistercian manuscript illumination nevertheless reveals that, in the early days of the order during the abbacies of Alberic (1099–1109) and Stephen Harding (1109–1133), such work still displayed the contemporary taste for a variety of colors and motifs in the Cluniac vein. Bernard's principles only won out later, with the promulgation of a statute in 1152 advocating that initial letters be executed in a non-figurative, monochromatic style. Assuming a strict parallel in architecture, it is therefore possible that Bernard's comments were initially aimed at an early version of Cistercian sculpture that has not survived.

The argument of the *Apologia* was basically pitched at the level of discipline rather than philosophy or aesthetics. Bernard did not condemn such sculpture for being ugly. The chiasmic expression "deformed beauty and beautiful deformity" (*deformis formositas ac formosa deformitas*) even hints at a positive value judgment. Nor did Bernard reject such creatures because they came straight from the demonic world of delirium or ancient mythology divorced from the Christian universe. Nor did he credit them with allegorical impact; such carvings represent nothing other than themselves—which is worth noting, given the highly common tendency toward symbolism. These freakish images were to be banned from cloisters because they distracted monks from spiritual activity, because they diverted the brethren from *lectio divina* (divine study). The seductive power of such images was too strong and dangerous not to lead to sin. In the end, Bernard's comments reveal a concern for discipline identical to the one found in customaries that sought to avoid giving monks occasions to stare, distract their neighbors, daydream, or fall asleep.

It should be noted that at no point did Bernard describe a human, divine, or angelic figure, or a story inspired by the Bible. The beginning of his *Apologia*, devoted to abuses in the church itself, did raise the issue of figurative pavements that bore images of saints or angels, trodden underfoot. "Often they spit on the face of an angel, often passers-by step on the faces of saints." Here again, the scandal is not the fashioning of the image, but its irreverent placement. He did not return to this argument for the cloisters.

Bernard's hostility therefore spared figurative sculpture that might be called Christian in theme. Ever since Gregory the Great wrote a famous letter to the iconoclast bishop Serenus of Marseilles around 600, in which the pope defended the educational role of paintings (described as "a Bible for the unlettered"), the Western church granted a special role to Christian imagery. And Bernard seemed to be aware of this in his letter. Indeed, paintings of saints, narrative cycles, and sculpture on historiated capitals could, in their own way, replace the monks' sacred readings, serving as a focus of meditation and edification. In order to eliminate, for reasons of principle, all figurative representation, Bernard the skillful debater therefore avoided raising the issue of such Christian imagery, protected as it was by Western tradition. As an advocate of cloisters that were aniconic (that is to say, free of human or animal forms)—indeed, totally devoid of representational imagery—Bernard disparaged all figurative decoration in an effort to elevate the monks' contemplative life.

A world of imagery

The capitals of the columns in cloisters offered a prime surface for decoration, whether ornamental or figurative. Figurative capitals made their appearance in the Romanesque period, then disappeared along with it. Earlier, almost no figurative motifs had been carved into Carolingian capitals, which were cubic or foliate. And following the Romanesque era, Gothic capitals returned to a purely foliate and stylized mode. In the Renaissance, meanwhile, capitals imitated the ancient Roman orders or were reduced to a simple abacus (square slab) on top of the column. The story of figurative capitals therefore really began in the eleventh century with experiments that combined foliate, geometric, and animal motifs in the form of facing figures arranged in mir-

ror symmetry on the base of the capital. By 1030, as a look at the porch at Saint-Benoît-sur-Loire shows, sculptors were cutting back on luxuriant vegetation in order to give more room to the figures alone, depicting Christian episodes from the Bible and lives of saints, thereby leading to narrative or "historiated" capitals. The oldest cloister in France to display historiated capitals is found at the Benedictine abbey of Moissac. Built in 1100 during the abbacy of Ansquitil, it combines forty-five historiated capitals with eleven capitals featuring figurative subjects (birds, dragons) and twenty others with foliate patterns (pp. 162-163). The cloister thus mingles Christian figures, non-Christian figures (which might nevertheless be Christianized through symbolism), and stylized foliage, establishing the three decorative approaches adopted by Romanesque cloisters.

By the second quarter of the twelfth century, just when the sculpting of capitals was at its height, confidently extending over the entire surface of the block, the Cistercian reaction proposed another stylistic path open to modern techniques, yet based on a willful return to pre-Romanesque forms. Did the Cistercians, forerunners of the Gothic technique of ribbed vaults, thereby contribute to the death of historiated capitals? As early as 1140, apparently, the limited space on capitals—initially a source of inspiration—began to be perceived as a hindrance by sculptors who sought to free themselves in order to deal with the vaster surfaces of facades. Historiated capitals therefore began to go into decline, almost totally dying out by the end of the twelfth century.

During the Romanesque era, figurative decoration invaded everything like over-exuberant plant growth. Although capitals were its focal point, such decoration spread to all kinds of surfaces: cornices, the tops of arches, the middle of spandrels between arches, on consoles, and even on the shafts of columns. Sculpture neverthe-

FANCIFUL MONSTER, MONTMAJOUR (FRANCE).

less gave way to painting on wooden ceilings and the gallery walls. In southern Italy, it was replaced by mosaics. Romanesque art thus called for a radical decorative choice, opting either for a completely historiated effect or the total austerity of the Cistercians, with no middle path. In the later Gothic period, when foliage became king, the keystones of vaults, where the ribs met, still continued to provide flat surfaces that welcomed figurative decoration.

Starting in the late thirteenth century, historiated stained glass might be set in the arcades, especially in northern Europe; sometimes only the upper tracery of stone was glazed (Canterbury, p. 60), sometimes the entire opening was glassed in, separating the gallery from the courtyard it surrounded (Gloucester, p. 118). This painted glass repeated the role and subject-matter of wall paintings. Some Cistercian cloisters, replacing Bernard's aniconic principles with art's pedagogical purpose, presented tales from the life of the saintly abbot for the monks' own edification (for example at Wettingen in Switzerland).

The wall painting done in cloisters in the high Middle Ages has sadly disappeared, the weather having worn away all decoration. Surviving examples are all posterior to the building of the galleries, such as the Renaissance cloisters in southern Europe (the green cloister of Santa Maria Novella in Florence, and Monte Oliveto Maggiore near Siena). Late examples—Santa Cruz in Coimbra (sixteenth century), Santa Chiara in Naples and the cathedral of Porto (eighteenth century)—employed painted tiles to present secular or mythological scenes, which meant that the cloister had become merely an excuse for decorative whimsy. A veritable divergence was created between the religious purpose of the architecture and the choice of imagery.

Every cloister must therefore be viewed individually as a place where artists, depending on period taste and local specificity, might utilize diverse, unexpected supports for figurative decoration.

A CLOISTER IN ALL ITS FINERY

Casting shadows

By playing on shadow and light, the architecture of a cloister dresses itself in fleeting, ever-changing finery. Like the rhythmic life of monks and canons, such decoration is intimately governed by variations in weather and time of day. Depending on the way a wall faces, the sun will strike it more or less directly—sometimes sunlight climbs to the top of a wall, sometimes it drops to the ground; depending on the carving that fills the arcades, such light may be geometric or flamboyant, fragmented or solid.

The infilling between the openings of an arcade therefore plays a double decorative role: it is both an ornamental surface and filtering screen. In the Cistercian cloister at Le Thoronet (France), completed prior to 1200, the Romanesque masonry divides the main arch into two bays, above which was a type of infilling called a "form-piece" with a round window soberly cut into it (p. 34). Thick as a wall, it keeps the galleries cool and meditative, shielded from the hot southern sun. Cistercian abbeys in Sénanque and Silvacane (both in Provence), and Fontfroide (southeast France) retained this aesthetic of protective solidity even as they lightened it. The cloister at Sénanque, built in the late twelfth century, has massive piers defining three-bay arches containing slim twinned columns that share a single abacus (p. 88). Fontfroide, meanwhile, represents a synthesis of two successive periods: the form-pieces, cleanly pierced by one or three round windows, are of Romanesque sobriety, while the pointed arches of the high bays and the svelte columns with foliate capitals betray Gothic refinements of the mid thirteenth century. Similar approaches were followed deep into the Gothic period, for example the cloister at the Portuguese cathedral of Porto, built in the fourteenth century. The huge round window set under the pointed main arch lends it an impressive severity, now tempered by the striking blue tiles, known as azulejos, added around 1730 (p. 103).

During the Gothic period, the upper form-piece of the main arch became more complex and fragmented. Adopting curvilinear motifs within each bay, it became known as tracery. Among the Cistercians of Noirlac, the sober tracery in the cloister comprised twinned pointed arches crowned either by a round window (in the standard "Chartres" or "Soissons" manner) or a trefoil set in a curved triangle (p. 27). Other possibilities were developed: quatrefoils with round or pointed lobes, arranged in a cross or X pattern within circles or bulging squares; extensive openwork in the spandrels (the curvilinear triangles between the arches) and other solid surfaces; lancet arches with trefoil or polyfoil cusping, also with openwork. Gothic tracery was refined into a geometric lattice in the thirteenth century, becoming ever lighter and more ethereal in the fourteenth.

The Cistercian cloister of Poblet in Catalonia, whose construction lasted more than a century, betrays such evolution. One gallery and the lavabo (or fountain for ablutions), both dating from the 1200s, have a simple form-piece with a diamond-shaped window over the two bays. The other three galleries, from the early fourteenth century, adopted fashionable quatrefoil tracery even as they avoided the mannerism of the 1300s out of faithfulness to the Cistercian ideal of a retrograde aesthetic (pp. 106-107). In the sister abbey of Santes Creus, also Cistercian, the sections built between 1303 and 1341 show how a desire for an archaic robustness gave way to a lace-like cloister (pp. 124-125). The cloister at Lérida, still in Catalonia, completed in the fourteenth century, displays several original features: it is located in front of the old cathedral, like a forecourt; its western gallery opens on two sides, giving onto both the inner courtyard and the outer walls, leading to the infinite space of the plain beyond the twin curtains of stone.

Slim lancet arches cast shadows on the flooring, suggesting a ghostly procession of hooded monks, with the tracery above their heads forming a constellation of three- and four-branched stars. The regularity of geometric tracery was broken in the fifteenth century with the arrival of the flamboyant style that elongated or compressed shapes, inventing two new, highly elastic shapes, called a *soufflet* and a *mouchette*. A soufflet extends the quatrefoil pattern by alternately rounding and pointing its lobes, while a mouchette is a languid dagger shape that can bend and flicker like a flame. This type of tracery was therefore dubbed "flamboyant" in France, which also became the name for Late French Gothic architecture in general.

This repertoire was conjugated in the Carthusian monastery of Saint-Sauveur in Villefranche-de-Rouergue (France), with its little cloister of 1459 placed next to the church. The tracery above the bays features a central soufflet surrounded by a riot of curling mouchettes, diamonds, and almond shapes (p. 126). At the late-fifteenth-century Cistercian cloister of La Oliva in Pamplona (Spain), two pairs of mouchettes swirl in a spiraling movement that locks them in a mad dance (p. 127).

In the Dominican cloister of Batalha (Portugal), designed circa 1388, the tracery developed around 1500 by architect Diogo Boytac generated a new field of experimentation distantly based on flamboyant Gothic (whose principles were barely apparent). The new style, straddling the late Middle Ages and the modern era, was called Manueline, in homage to King Manuel I the Great (1495–1521). Tracery was handled like a festooned screen or blind—the web became so dense that openwork no longer dialogued with substance on an equal footing, but instead underscored the ornamental composition. The aesthetic of voids, so dear to flamboyant, had given way to an aesthetic of solids.

Sublimating nature

If four sides of the allegorical cloister automatically evoked the tetrad of elements making up the universe (earth, air, fire, water), certain natural sites lent true vigor to this symbolism. At Mont-Saint-Michel in France, for instance, the sleek dark columns erected between sky and sea in 1228 preside over the visual encounter of those two blue vastnesses (pp. 104-105). In order to withstand the violent coalition of wind and waves, the columns take root, like serried plants, in a staggered double row. The oceanic cloister of Mont-Saint-Michel is mirrored by troglodytic one of San Juan de la Peña (Spain). Built between 1189 and 1201 below the powerful jaws of a cliff, it has only the overhanging rock for a roof. The Catalonian cloister of Lérida, meanwhile, perched on the tip of a promontory, seems ready to take flight whereas Saint Martin, set in the ravined outcrops of Mount Canigou, appears happy to nestle there. Whether whipped by the wind or sheltered by rock, these seaside and mountainside cloisters confront

a wild, hostile nature recalling the wilderness confronted by the earliest monks.

Once inside the cloister, nature is tamed and stylized, becoming part of the décor. Water, vegetation, and stone are joined together by human handicraft. For ritual ablutions, the Cistercians were the first to design a special pavilion for the lavabo, projecting from one of the galleries. Like the fountain it houses, this pavilion was often circular (or polygonal) in plan, breaking the regular quadrangle of the cloister (at Poblet (p. 55) and Le Thoronet and Alcobaça, p. 57). Or it might take quadrangular form among the Sicilian Benedictines of Monreale (1172–1189) and the Portuguese Dominicans of Batalha (after 1402). Extending into the courtyard like a figurehead, becoming a cloister within the cloister, the lavabo pavilion multiplied the number of viewpoints and complicated the weave of columns.

Certain columns were handled in a way that transcended the conventional analogy with a tree trunk. The botanical repertoire was in fact limitless—the sculptor at Monreale simply imitated the coarse, chevroned stems of Sicilian palms (p. 112). At the cloister of Saint John Lateran (Rome, 1215–1236), wiry vines spiral up the marble. Some columns even abandoned their functional verticality: on the northwest pier of the cloister in Aix-en-Provence (France), built in the years 1190–1200, four twinned columns bend their supple shafts halfway up, skirt to the left, and only rejoin the Corinthian capital at the next corner (p. 2). At Santo Domingo de Silos (Spain), the imposing weight of one historiated capital in the north wing (1085–1100) induces the column to slant and shift, though not to bend (p. 164).

The natural, foliate effect of tracery, meanwhile, was underscored by relief carving. In the northern Spanish cloister of La Oliva, curved molding (called a torus) swells as though sap were rising through it; it springs from the top of the mullions (where vine leaves and a bunch of grapes sprout, p. 32), then branches higher

LA OLIVA (SPAIN).

into vigorous stems on the flamboyant trellis (p. 127). In the little Carthusian cloister at Villefranche-de-Rouergue (France), master builder Jean Coupiac (1451–1459) decided instead to grow frilly cabbage on the hanging pendants of the tracery. Meanwhile, the Manueline tracery in the cloister of Batalha forms prickly hedges: bare shoots entwine the cross of the military Order of Christ, while thorny branches surround Manuel I's armillary sphere (pp. 33, 112).

Invasive vegetation grew up columns in limitless variety—ivy, grapevines, pine cones, intertwining ferns, four-leaf clover, palmettes, stylized foliate scrolls, all kinds of whimsical aborescence. Fooled by this illusionist game, animals sometimes alight there, such as the pheasants at Monreale glimpsed pecking at scrolls of foliage on a capital (p. 44).

The play of polychrome

Monochrome cloisters were rare; even in the absence of painted features, the stone itself provided color. The use of marble or marble-like limestone for the shafts of columns offered a broad range of tones that could be brightly polished. Witness the pink cloister at Saint-Michel-de-Cuxa (France), erected in 1125–1137 during the abbacy of Grégoire (p. 10); or the bluish cloister of Elne (France), built between the twelfth and fourteenth centuries; or the purple and gray cloister of Mont-Saint-Michel, a "wonder" that employed both Purbeck marble (a marble-like stone from England) and limestone (p. 67).

The combination of brick and volcanic rock from Auvergne in central France produced fascinating effects in the cloister at Le Puy (twelfth century). Black and gray lava, ocher and orange bricks, and off-white terracotta were coordinated with regularity that escaped monotony as the polychrome geometry wedded architectural shapes (pp. 96-97) The stone-cutting and the variety of layered string courses amplified this play of

BATALHA (PORTUGAL).

color: the voussoirs of the arches were set in a radial position, angled diamonds were used for the string-course, a net-like pattern filled the spandrels, and parallelograms produced a pleated ribbon effect. The whole ensemble was finally structured by the thick dividing lines of false red-brick joins.

Sicily, another volcanic region, provided the cloister of Monreale with the gray lava used as inlay along its arcade—circles, oblong and equilateral triangles, diamond-shapes, and chevrons are outlined with pale mortar (p. 97). This inlay represents a kind of heraldic decoration in honor of King William II (1166–1189). Few of the cloister's 114 pairs of columns orchestrating the perfect square (47 by 47 meters) are repeated. Some are smooth, other carved with geometric, foliate, or figurative motifs, many are covered in mosaics. The largely gold tesserae, combined with blue, red, white, and black fragments, sparkle magnificently against the whiteness of the marble (p. 82).

This marriage of hard stone with glass-paste mosaic spread to Rome and throughout southern Italy in the twelfth century, covering floors, pulpits, and altar canopies in a pattern now known as Cosmati work. The Cosmati were a group of architectural marble workers—many coming from families named Cosma—who shared this taste for inlay, popular from the early twelfth to the late thirteenth century. In Rome the two main Cosmati cloisters, San Paolo fuori le Mure and Saint John Lateran were ascribed to the Vassalletto family, who completed them in 1214 and 1236 respectively. Various types of columns were aligned without rhyme or reason, in a heady visual combination: smooth, twisted, cabled, spiral, plain and heavily gilded (p. 83). In San Paolo, a straight column (inlaid with chevrons that alternate with stripes) is set next to a fluted, twisting one (pp. 80-81); on the first column, the geometric tesserae tolerate constantly evolving patterns, while on the second column four intertwining ribbons follow repetitive patterns that re-assert a regular rhythm. Light spills across this twisted shaft, tripping haphazardly from ring to ring.

In other climes, at other times, cloisters were endowed with color from painted ceramics. At Santa Cruz de Coimbra (Portugal), built between 1517 and 1521 by Marques Pirès in the Manueline style, the lower walls of the galleries were decorated with blue and white azulejos against a yellow ground (p. 21). In Naples, the cloister of the nuns of Santa Chiara was transformed with floral majolica work by Domenico Antonio Vaccaro in 1741–1742 (pp. 100-101).

Cloisters and Islam

In Spain and southern Italy, the idiom of Islamic art left its traces even in cloisters. The Catholic reconquest of the Iberian peninsula, which began in the ninth century, encompassed the former kingdoms of Saragossa, Toledo, and Al-Andalous by the late thirteenth century. Only the kingdom of Grenada, on the southern tip of

Spain, maintained an Islamic political presence up to 1492. The "mudéjar" style, named after Muslims who remained in territories reconquered by Christians, reveals the survival of Islamic taste in those regions, regardless of the religion or status of artist and patron. The little town of Soria, on the border of the kingdoms of Saragossa and Castille, hosted a monastery, Aranda de Duero, built by the military order of the Hospitalers of Saint John of Jerusalem, founded in 1113 in the Holy Land—an order inspired by both the Benedictine and the Augustinian rules; the cloister, dating from around 1200, featured a surprising melange of arcades—a garland of pointed horseshoe arches, overlapping and intertwining in mudéjar fashion, is all that remains in the grassy ruins (p. 69).

The typically Iberian order of Saint Hieronymus (Jerome), founded by two Spanish hermits in 1373 under the Rule of Saint Augustine, was given charge of the church of the Virgin of Guadalupe, which became a major pilgrimage site in the fourteenth century. The large cloister of this Hieronymite monastery, founded in 1389, boasts a two-story gallery of horseshoe arches, more or less pointed, typical of mudéjar art (p. 61). In the middle of the courtyard, a pavilion dating from 1405 boldly combines Gothic features (lancet arches, slim columns) with a lacy polygonal tower.

In the city of Toledo itself, the Franciscan cloister of San Juan de los Reyes, founded in 1476, also presents two opposing styles on two levels; the lower gallery is late Gothic in style, while the upper gallery has mudéjar connotations with its multi-curved arches and ceiling of painted wood (pp. 98-99).

In Italy, Sicily was under Fatimid control between the ninth and eleventh centuries, until it was conquered by Normans Roger I and Robert Guiscard, who also seized lands on the southern tip of the peninsula. The art of the new Norman kingdom was steeped in all the Byzantine, Arab, and Latin influences that had flourished there. Thus at Amalfi (which had trade links to the Arab kingdoms, and was annexed by Sicily), the cathedral cloister, built between 1266 and 1268, borrowed the Islamic penchant for narrow, pointed horseshoe arches, aligned in twos, threes, and fours beneath blind, interleaved arcs (pp. 110-111).

Evolutions in vaulting

The stylistic and technical developments in ceiling vaults that occurred between the eleventh and sixteenth centuries weighed upon the otherwise unchanged structure of the four-sided cloister. The Romanesque period was characterized by several types of vault. A few cloisters still retain flat ceilings of wood, the oldest way of covering the galleries. The most typical vault, however, was the semi-cylindrical barrel vault that ran the length of the gallery, either unbroken or divided into bays by transverse arches. In the cloisters at Sénanque and Silvacane, the sectioned barrel vault had a semi-circular curve whereas at Le Thoronet it is slightly pointed.

A simple, austere harmony is generated by the union of these sheltering vaults with the massive arcades and rounded archways of the bays. But the twelfth century also offered another model, namely groin vaults, as seen in the cathedral cloister at Le Puy. In theory, this vaulting was produced by the intersection at right angles of two barrel vaults of identical shape, yielding two diagonal counter arches that crisscrossed in the middle, their ridges clearly orchestrating the rhythm of the gallery (p. 66). Cistercian monasteries, finally, displayed equal mastery over barrel vaults and early ribbed vaults. Until the thirteenth century, however, ribbed vaulting was used only for the chapter-house; a concern for austerity meant that barrel vaults continued to be used for the abbey church and most other buildings. The plan of this simple ribbed vault was the same as a groin vault, except that the marked ribbing reinforced the simple ridges of the crisscrossing counter arches. The ribs ran diagonally across the vault to the keystone in the middle, where they met their opposite numbers.

Rib vaults are associated with Gothic architecture.

LE THORONET (FRANCE).

ROYAUMONT (FRANCE).

The three galleries of the cloister of Royaumont (France) illustrate the "rayonnant" style that emerged around Paris during the reign of Louis IX (1226–1270). Royaumont, as its royal name suggest, was founded by the king in 1228 as a place of eternal rest for the remains of the royal family. Affiliated with the Cistercian order, the monastery combined Cistercian austerity with the nobility of the royal founders. The vault's ribs are presented in all their purity, generously lit by bays with no infilling (p. 34). Solid piers, elegantly ringed by slim shafts, receive the diagonal ribs on the courtyard side, while on the wall side the ribs spring from corbels decorated with crockets.

Anthology of ribbing

Once rib vaults came to dominate Europe from the thirteenth century onward, rival experiments in ribbing led to great technical and aesthetic refinements. In the first instance, these refinements concerned arch moldings (convex torus, concave ovolo, chamfered, flat fillets, semi-oval scotias, etc.) and complex combinations of moldings (S-shaped cyma recta, prismatic moldings, etc). Furthermore, the vault was enriched with additional ribs, notably tiercerons and liernes, whose role was above all decorative. The tierceron is a secondary rib that springs from one of the main springers, but instead of running to the keystone runs to the ridge-rib, where it is met by a symmetrical tierceron. A lierne is a tertiary rib that does not spring either from a main springer or the central boss, but usually from a transverse rib, although it can sometimes link the bosses of tiercerons to the keystone boss, as seen at the flamboyant-style, post-1468 cloister of Cadouin in France (p. 35). In contrast, the Franciscan cloister of San Juan de los Reyes in Toledo eliminated ribs in favor of complementary arches alone, which frame the central ceiling of the vault, devoid of bosses. Decorative exuberance produced its richest specimens in the Manueline style. At the Hieronymite monastery of Belém, near Lisbon, the beauty of the 1517 cloister resides in its baroque extremes—reticulated vaults laden with carved bosses, arches with cusped undersides, columns and embrasures loaded with stylized vegetation, tracery worked in foliate clusters, and so on (pp. 128-129).

As a finale, two examples from England: in the cathedral cloister of Norwich—built between 1297 and 1430 and thereby covering all stages of English Gothic—a superb lierne runs the length of the vault, carved with polychrome figures at each point of junction (pp. 160–161). The abundance of complementary ribs, the choice of prismatic moldings with multiple facets, and the ornamentation of bosses produces an effect of profusion corresponding to what was called the "decorated style."

Around 1330, the decorated style gave way to the perpendicular style. The first example of perpendicular style can be seen in the Benedictine abbey of Gloucester, renovated from 1337 onwards. The style takes its name from the systematic use of rectangular panels to fill the bays, unifying the overall effect and making it possible to set glass into large open-work surfaces. In the cloister at Gloucester (1360–1370), the ceiling is composed of fan-vaults based on inverted half-cones (p. 118). The ribbing combines the effect of perpendicular tracery with a need to arrange it along the arc of a circle, producing the effect of petals or the rays of a large rose-window (p. 123). The flat surfaces of the ceiling are decorated with circles and cusped polyfoils. The fan structure and dense ribbing of these vaults, set along endlessly repeating bays, generates a heady impression of movement and undulation. The microcosm of the cloister, designed to detach itself from the world, thus created its own heavens.

CADOUIN (FRANCE).

With four galleries leading from one into another endlessly, a cloister is highly suited to the depiction of continuous visual discourse, to the appreciation of painted or carved narratives on walls, ceilings, and capitals. This concept was embodied by historiated cloisters during the Romanesque era of the eleventh and twelfth centuries (along with a few later examples). The progression of a stroll beneath a portico has perhaps been an active metaphor for discourse since the days of peripatetic philosophers at the Lyceum. A historiated cloister is a four-page book which a stroller might read in one go or peruse sequence by sequence, going from one wing to another, pausing or dawdling to peruse again. Such discursiveness, however, is not geared to a gradual, carefully constructed and completed argument. The book of the cloister can be opened at any point and closed at any point. It can be explored in one direction or the other. Its impact stems from breaks in narration, from changes in tone, from repetition and ultimately total reiteration. This impression may stem from the disappearance of almost all painted decoration liable to guide and comment on the sculpted decoration, but whatever the case a historiated cloister remains, for us, structured around a contradiction: it was spatially emblematic of narrative progression, yet was not subject to the rules of continuous discourse. It was an open book written by several authors, to be perused in several directions and understood in more than one way.

NARRATIVE DECORATION

Historiated capitals

The structure of a capital is admirably suited to the narrative nature of sculpture. Like the cloister itself, a capital has four sides that cannot be seen simultaneously, thereby requiring progressive movement.

A medieval capital was composed of several elements: the main body (called the cushion or echinus), a crowning slab (abacus), and a molding around its base (sometimes called astragal) to mark the separation between the shaft of the column and the capital. In ancient architecture the astragal had been part of the shaft, whereas in medieval architecture it became part of the capital. A capital might take various forms, depending on its size and the number of columns supporting it. The conical or upside-down pyramidal shape was the most common. In Romanesque cloisters, variety was important. When the supporting shafts were smaller and twinned, the two capitals would be combined into one body, crowned by a single abacus. At Monreale, for example, each capital retains three of its sides, while the fourth

merges with its neighbor (p. 44). This created a double capital conceived as a surface with two times three sides. At Moissac, however, where single and twin columns alternate, the doubling of the capital is barely noticeable because it always results in a single cushion with four sides (p. 36). The now-demolished cloister of La Daurade in Toulouse provided an example of triple capitals that merged into a single body at mid-height. At Silos, four columns support the capitals in the middle of the galleries, and at these spots the capital is unified into a single, immense body. Such differences appeared within the same series, for they allowed sculptors to modulate their compositions, enlarging them for a combined body or, on the contrary, tightening them for a single capital.

The text of a capital unfolds in time and space like the text of a book or—to retain the metaphor of circular motion—like a parchment scroll. For example, the west wing of the Monreale cloister has a double capital that recounts six episodes from Genesis: three sides of one capital show Original Sin, Adam and Eve expulsed from Eden, and their subsequent labor, while the three sides of the other capital depict the sacrifice of Cain and Abel followed by their respective deaths. This arrangement of the imagery mimics the spatial and chronological progression of the tale.

Even though the structure of a capital is conducive to narration, like a cloister it raises a certain number of contradictions that will be briefly discussed here. For instance, the point at which the "reading" begins often varies, sometimes starting on the narrow outer side,

Moissac (France).

other times on the lateral side, and so on. Nor is the direction of reading always uniform; even when four scenes are chronologically linked, two will often read from left to right while the following two only make sense if read from right to left, or else the order may be reversed on a neighboring capital. Historiated capitals were thus composed of heterogeneous parameters— intermittent versus sequential, discontinuous versus narrational—which disturb conventional notions of discursiveness.

Historiated piers

A chronological series of three Romanesque cloisters— Moissac, Silos, and Arles—offers the possibility of analyzing the principles behind historiated piers. All three examples concern substantial pillars rather than slender columns. The cloister of Saint-Pierre in Moissac (France) testifies to the practice of sculpting the four corner piers and the central piers in each wing (two of which have survived, in the east and north galleries). Full-length figures, some five feet high, were carved in bas-relief on thin slabs of marble, probably salvaged from ancient sarcophagi (pp. 162-163). Identifiable figures include apostles Peter and Paul (southeast pier), James and John (northeast pier), Philip and Andrew (northwest pier), and Bartholomew and Matthew (southwest pier). Simon can be found on the outer face (garden side) of the central pillar of the west wing, while the inner face bears an inscription making it possible to date construction of the cloister to 1100 or thereabouts. A half century later, at San Domingo in Silos (Spain), the principle of the sculpted corner pier was taken up and used as a narrative medium for recounting the final episodes in Christ's earthly life, from the Passion to Pentecost. Any similarity with a funeral slab, still highly present at Moissac, has now disappeared. The carving tells a story and composes a tableau framed by two lateral columns and an overhead arch (pp. 164-179).

THE ROAD TO EMMAUS AND DOUBTING THOMAS, PIER, SANTO DOMINGO DE SILOS (SPAIN).

The corner piers at Saint-Trophime in Arles (France), located in the Romanesque part of the cloister (1080–1120), represent a synthesis of the two approaches at Moissac and Silos by juxtaposing full-length figures with historiated reliefs. The full-length figures are once again apostles, but they in no way resemble the attenuated relief figures seen at Moissac. The apostles at Arles are veritable statues, carved in high relief and free in movement. They flank historiated plaques recounting related stories. On the northwest corner, for example, Saints John the Evangelist and Trophime frame the story of Holy Women who came to buy spices from merchants; according to legend, these Holy Women were none other than the Marys who, with their brother Lazarus, arrived on the Mediterranean coasts of Provence where they were met by Trophime.

An historiated pier, unlike a capital, can be taken in with one glance. This simultaneity made it possible to combine statues and high reliefs at Arles. At Silos, the narrative sculptures form isolated ensembles that demand no progressive movement on the part of the viewer. Only the relief showing the Road to Emmaus, in which the striding Christ indicates movement beyond the frame, perhaps invites the gaze to turn (or return) to the neighboring face. Globally, it could be said that each scene enjoys autonomy within the visual narration.

Independent surfaces

Although capitals and corner piers account for most relief sculpture in a Romanesque cloister, other surfaces may flesh out the visual text of the decorative scheme. The problem is to understand how they fit into the narrative thread. Often, such sculpture concerns freakish heads that regularly appear on highly worked cornices, as can be seen in the cloisters of Le Puy (p. 97) and San Paolo fuori le Mura (pp. 84-85).

The triangular spandrels between arches offered another potential surface. At San Paolo fuori le Mura, the repetition of subjects (a man or a tree caught between demonic animals) suggest they should be read as a frieze. In the Arles cloister, however, only the east wing has carved spandrels, which show, respectively, the evangelists in their symbolic animal forms (angel, lion, bull, and eagle), two grotesque heads, and the ten wise and foolish virgins—a sequence that is hard to explain. Or should we be looking for a vertical connection between, say, capital and spandrel or between spandrel and a hypothetical painted surface? On these independent, repetitious surfaces, subjects only assume meaning in groups, calling for new visual categories.

Even as historiated capitals were being abandoned by Gothic sculptors, it was not unusual to find bases, bosses, and balustrades that still bore figures in the late Middle Ages. The historiated bosses in the English cloister of Norwich are polychrome in a way that faithfully conveys the original appearance of most sculptures, which time has stripped of this crucial apparel (pp. 160-161). Their subjects include Christ in Majesty displaying

His wounds, phantasmagorical creatures, courtly and mercantile scenes. No apparent iconography links these subjects, and there is a great distance between the bosses (not to mention the distance from the eye below, trying to discern all the details). Finally, on the threshold of the Renaissance, relief medallions at Santa Maria Huerta—pairing prophets with apostles—provide one last testimony to such profuse decoration (pp. 138-139).

SACRED READINGS, SECULAR READINGS

Illustrating the Bible

Historiated capitals were an extension of the reading done by monks, a reflection of their *lectio divina*, an echo of their psalmody. Such capitals therefore delved into the repertoire of the Old and New Testaments. Adam and Eve, our earliest forbears, are often shown in their nakedness around the Tree of Life (Genesis 3: 1–8). The depiction of this single moment, on its own, sufficed to signify the entire creation story, from Adam being formed from dust to the couple's expulsion from the Garden of Eden (the end of Genesis 3). At Moissac and Monreale, the scene of original sin is accompanied by other episodes: the Lord reproaching the couple who become aware of their nudity, driving them from Eden, Eve working at the distaff, and Adam hoeing the soil. The consequences of their sin falls on their sons (Genesis 4)—the antagonism between Cain the tiller (whose offering did not please God) and Abel the shepherd finally ended in fratricide. It is easy to recognize Cain, whose arm is raised to strike his brother with his club.

Reminding viewers of the Fall was designed to underscore the evil that corrupted mankind from its origins, placing humanity's own sin before the monks' eyes every day; at the same time, it also evoked, through a typological interpretation of prefiguration, man's redemption by Christ. Typology (from the Greek *typos*, imprint) was a common method of Christian exegesis that involved interpreting an event from the Old Testament as a prefiguration of an event in the New, as an obscure incident that could only be understood in full light once Christ arrived. Thus Christ was called the new Adam, and Mary the new Eve, because sin contains the seed of salvation.

The story of Abraham, often found on capitals, signified more than the straightforward tale. The patriarch Abraham was the image par excellence of a man of faith who blindly followed divine instructions and who believed unshakably in divine promises even when unrealistic, contradictory, or scandalous. Abraham and Sarah, despite their great age, longed for the son announced by three angels at the oaks of Mamre (Genesis 18); even though God promised to "multiply [Abraham's] descendents as the stars of heaven," Abraham was prepared to sacrifice his only son, young Isaac, at God's request (Genesis 22). According to a typological interpretation, the sacrifice of Isaac represents more than Abraham's extraordinary act—it prefigures the sacrifice of Christ as innocent victim. Christ is Isaac (who himself carried the bundle of wood for the burnt offering), carrying his own cross of torture and consenting to mount the altar of sacrifice. At the same time, Christ was also the ram caught in the bush that God sent Abraham to replace Isaac, since God finally spared the son after having tested his father's faith.

Other Old Testament characters are stock figures in historiated sculpture, for example Noah, Joseph in Egypt, David and the giant Goliath, and David with the Queen of Sheba. Making no attempt at comprehensiveness, it is worth citing here the main heroes of the genre—namely Samson, Daniel in the Lions' Den, and the three Hebrews in the fiery furnace (Shadrach, Meshach, and Abednego). The youth, strength, and faith of these biblical figures was sorely tried, but they

TWO VERSIONS OF DANIEL IN THE LIONS' DEN: NORTH GALLERY (*RIGHT*) AND WEST GALLERY (*LEFT*, DETAIL), MOISSAC (FRANCE).

all emerged victorious with God's help.

Samson, who appears in the book of Judges (chaps. 13–16), incarnates physical strength—he tore a lion asunder with his bare hands, and slayed one thousand Philistines with the jawbone of an ass. A capital at Monreale shows Samson in Gaza, where he had followed a harlot. Nude in her bed, she clings to his garment while the local people, preparing to kill Samson, shut the gates of the city (p. 158). But Samson rose in the middle of the night and pulled out the posts of the gate, then carried them up to the top of a mountain. On a capital in Arles, he is shown with Delilah, who entices him to reveal the secret of his invincibility in order to deliver him to the Philistines. Unmatched strength thus gave way to total weakness: head shaven, eyes gouged out, Samson is shown turning a mill like a beast of burden. But his hair grew back, his strength returned, and he avenged himself by pulling down two columns supporting a temple filled with Philistines, dying along with them as the roof collapsed. The story of Samson is rich in lessons: a moral lesson on the invincible strength of believers, and a typological lesson on Christ who suffered the affronts of the Passion only to rise again and win a final victory over evil. In order to associate Christ with Samson, the latter's incongruous immorality and conceit were simply overlooked, because the point was not to assert that Jesus Christ was another Samson, but rather that certain incidents in Samson's life prefigured certain motifs of salvation. This analytical method was traditional among commentators, and thus not unique to the carvers at Monreale.

The stories of Daniel in the Lions' Den and the Three Hebrews in the Furnace are connected because both are recounted in the book of Daniel (3: 1–23, 6: 1-28, and 14: 31–40), and both took place in Babylon during the reigns of the kings Nebuchadnezzar, Darius, and Cyrus. The underlying issues were recognition by the Babylonian government of exiled Hebrews and their

rise to power there. Daniel obtained Nebuchadnezzar's favor by interpreting a dream; the three other Hebrews, meanwhile—Shadrach, Meshach, and Abednego—were removed from their administrative posts for having refused to worship an idol. Thrown into a furnace, they survived unscathed by singing a hymn of thanksgiving. At Moissac, one capital shows them giving praise, arms outstretched, amid the flames—their heads have been broken off, but they remain identifiable thanks to inscriptions (p. 39). Daniel, whose piety also incurred royal wrath, was thrown into a den of lions. But God sent an angel and the lions spared Daniel (p. 38). In an apocryphal addition to the book of Daniel, the situation recurred under King Cyrus, when Daniel remained in the den for seven days, fed by the prophet Habakkuk who was transported from Judea every day by an angel; the incident concludes with the king's profession of faith. Iconological tradition often shows Daniel and the three Hebrews as youths, probably because their youthfulness suggests purity and reinforces the miracle of their steadfastness. From a typological standpoint, Daniel in the den prefigures Christ's Descent into Hell, followed by the Resurrection. From a moral standpoint, all four men illustrate the power of faith and prayer in the face of trials. For monks who knew the psalms by heart, such tribulations echoed the sorrow of the psalmist who sings even when his "soul [is] the midst of lions" (Psalm 57: 4, *Young's Literal Translation* [YLT]).

Christian mysteries: the Incarnation

New Testament subjects are among the most common to be found in cloister sculpture. Silos is an extreme example, being devoted exclusively to the New Testament at the expense of any depiction of the Old.

Two major themes were frequently featured—Christmas and Easter, representing the mysteries of Christ's Incarnation and his Passion and Resurrection. The Nativity cycle covered an extended period running not only from the Annunciation to the Adoration of the Magi (March 25 to the following January 6), but also to the Massacre of the Innocents and the Flight into Egypt, which supposedly occurred in the days following the Adoration of the Magi. The Annunciation was described in the gospel of Luke (1: 26–38), when the archangel Gabriel told Mary, a young woman from Nazareth betrothed to Joseph of the house of David, that she would conceive a son. Mary pragmatically pointed out that she had not yet known a man and was therefore still a virgin. "The Holy Spirit will come upon you," came the reply, "and the power of the Most High will overshadow you; therefore the child to be born will be called holy, the Son of God." A miracle if there ever was one, God thereby conceived a Son, and this Son was incarnated in flesh and blood—God become man. Theologically speaking, this was the greatest wonder of the whole episode—virginal conception was simultaneously a means and a proof. Mary acquiesced; the pact was signed; the angel departed.

THE HEBREWS IN THE FIERY FURNACE, CAPITAL, MOISSAC (FRANCE).

Gabriel's message also informed Mary that her aged and apparently barren cousin, Elizabeth the wife of Zachariah, was six-months pregnant. "For with God nothing will be impossible," he added, echoing the words of the angels of Mamre who promised the aging Sarah that she would give birth to Isaac (cf. Genesis 18: 14). Two miraculous conceptions inaugurated the new era: one concerned a virgin, the other a barren woman. Sculptures of the Annunciation were therefore naturally accompanied by the Visitation, that is to say the meeting of the two cousins, Mary and Elizabeth, confirming Gabriel's sibylline promises. Mary at this point was pregnant with Jesus, and Elizabeth immediately understood—or, at least, the babe in her own womb stirred and prompted Elizabeth to say: "Blessed are you among women, and blessed is the fruit of your womb. And why is this granted to me, that the mother of my Lord should come to me?" Mary, who had hardly spoken up till this point, then broke into a hymn of thanksgiving. In Romanesque painting and sculpture, this scene was portrayed as two women embracing, echoing the ubiquitous text of the psalmist and assuming almost cosmic value: "Kindness and truth have met, Righteousness and peace have kissed, Truth from the earth springeth up, And righteousness from heaven looketh out" (Psalm 85:10–11, *YLT*).

Then come scenes of the Nativity in Bethlehem. The young mother is shown reclining or half-sitting—it was only starting in the fourteenth century that she would be depicted kneeling in adoration of the child—while the newborn was swaddled nearby and Joseph pondered in one corner. The ox and the ass leaning over the child are apocryphal additions to the gospel, as are the two midwives bustling about the mother and washing the child. Named Zelomi and Salome, the two women did not assist Mary in the delivery—Mary supposedly gave birth alone, painlessly—but were there to attest to her true virginity, even postpartum. At Monreale, a capital at the northeast corner shows, side by the side, the Nativity presented by an angel who simultaneously points to the heavenly star beneath the abacus, and the announcement to the shepherds by another angel (or perhaps the same one, in an effort to indicate chronological development) who appeared to them with their dog and sheep (Luke 2: 8–20).

The tale of the Wise Men, or Magi, as recounted by Matthew (2: 1–12), might unfold over several scenes or, on the contrary, be condensed solely into the Adoration, or Epiphany. The Epiphany (from Greek *epiphaneia*, apparition) was interpreted as a theological climax, greater than the Nativity itself, because Jesus was here being recognized as King of the Jews, Shepherd of Israel. He was depicted as an infant-God. At first, the Magi from the East were just astronomers—or astrologers—who studied the stars and were alerted by the new, rising star. Tradition then turned them into kings, an allusion to Isaiah (60: 3) and Psalms 68 and 72 ("To thee do kings bring a present" 68:30, *YLT*). Their

number was commonly set at three. They might be shown before the Adoration, when passing through Jerusalem to visit Herod (who asked them to bring news of the child), as well as after the Adoration, when a dream warned them not to return to Herod. The Romanesque approach at Arles changed little at Elne, even though the long-limbed figures and pointed, three-lobed arches set the scene in an early-fourteenth-century Gothic arcade: the three Magi are still recognizable by their crowns, lying in one bed as an angel comes to warn them (p. 40). The Massacre of the Innocents, the direct consequence of Herod's alarm and anger, is shown alongside; on the instructions of Herod (whom the Elne sculptor showed sitting ignobly with one foot on his throne, elbow resting on the knee under his chin), a guard in a coat of mail stabs a naked infant held by the feet.

Christian mysteries: the Passion and Resurrection

Whereas the Nativity cycle covered a period of almost ten months, the Passion cycle lasted at most a week, from Christ's entry into Jerusalem (Palm Sunday) to Easter Sunday. It might often be limited to four days, the *biduum paschale*, starting with the Last Supper on Maundy (or Holy) Thursday. At Arles, the entry into Jerusalem runs all around one capital in the east gallery; the inner, least visible side (facing its twinned capital) shows the fortified architecture of a city with two inhabitants leaning from the ramparts, awaiting Christ. On the main side, three young people climb a tree and cut its branches, while below them another youth squats on his heels and spreads his cloak on the ground. Christ, riding a small donkey, is carved precisely on the left corner, his verticality underscoring the angular structure even as the donkey stresses horizontal movement (its forehooves are already stepping on the young man's cloak even as its hindquarters remain in the previous side). On the third and fourth sides, six apostles form Christ's procession, in two groups of three. The narrative aspect of this capital is therefore enhanced by the spatial and temporal development of

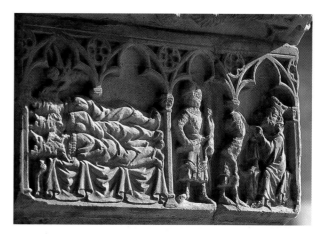

THE DREAM OF THE MAGI AND THE MASSACRE OF THE INNOCENTS, CAPITAL, ELNE (FRANCE).

the procession. Yet at the same time, the sculptor insured that it would have a messianic meaning by adding to the little donkey a lamb, *Agnus Dei*, as a reminder that death would soon follow the glory of Palm Sunday.

The Washing of the Disciples' Feet and the Last Supper took place on Thursday, the eve of preparations for the sabbath. The ablutions were described only in John (13: 1–16) who, for that matter, does not mention the consecration of the bread and wine. Almost all cloisters, for ritual reasons, depicted the Washing of the Disciples' Feet. At Moissac, Silos, and Arles this scene can be conventionally recognized by its two main characters: Christ with His cruciform halo (at least one knee on the ground and a towel knotted around His tunic), plus a disciple who bares his leg and prepares to place his foot in the basin of water on the ground. If this disciple is seen lifting his arm to touch his head with his hand, that means he is Saint Peter, visually alluding to his response when Jesus said, "If I do not wash you, you have no part in me." Peter replied, "Lord, not my feet only but also my hands and my head!"

This scene would be immediately followed by the Last Supper.

During the Romanesque period, the agony of the Passion was only a minor source of inspiration. It was not until the thirteenth century, spurred notably by Franciscan preaching about Christ's cross, that this subject was enthusiastically handled. The sculptor at Silos devoted one side of the northeast pillar to the Crucifixion, although the emphasis is already on the Descent from the Cross (p. 170). Christ is shown dead, eyes closed, head resting stiffly on His right shoulder. Two men, generally identified as Nicodemus and Joseph of Arimathea (John 19: 38–39), prepare to take Him down from the cross. The nail in Christ's right hand has already been removed, leaving a deep stigma. His left hand will soon be freed, and Joseph of

THE ENTOMBMENT, PIER, SANTO DOMINGO DE SILOS (SPAIN).

Arimathea extends his arms to receive the lifeless body. The men are flanked by Mary and John; Mary has taken the wounded hand of her son and presses it to her cheek, but John observes the scene without intervening. The book he holds indicates his role as witness; he provides proof of the incident, authenticating the sculpture as a truthful extension of the text of his gospel. God has died, and three angels rend the clouds to anoint the body with incense. God has died, and the sun and the moon are at His bedside—personified and sanctified by a halo, each figure holds a large cloth with his name (*Sol* and *Luna*). Their chests are covered, because the gospels reported that the sun veiled itself and that darkness prevailed between the sixth and ninth hours (noon and 3:00 p.m.). The apocryphal gospel of Peter stated that the light returned at the moment that the nails were drawn from the Lord's hands. At the same time, according to Peter, the earth quaked—so perhaps the stones underneath the feet of the figures in this scene are supposed to be rolling like waves. At the foot of the cross, one damaged figure lifts the slab of his sarcophagus, inscribed with the name of Adam: tradition held that Golgotha (or Calvary, the "place of skulls") was the mount where Seth placed the tomb of his father, Adam. Here then, typological concordance between the Old and New Testaments is fully at work. The wooden cross, depicted like a felled tree trunk, alludes to the Tree of Life that was denied to Adam by God after the Fall (Genesis 3: 22). By serving as a gallows for Christ, the Tree of Life was restored to mankind. The new Adam sacrificed himself so that the old Adam could rise from his grave. At Silos, this Descent from the Cross is matched, on the other side of the pier, by a relief that incorporates two distinct incidents, the Entombment and the Empty Tomb three days later (p. 41). The composition is structured by the horizontal slab on which Christ is laid and by the diagonal of the raised cover. In the middle, Joseph of Arimathea and Nicodemus are seen again, leaning over the corpse they have just set down. The thick slab, conceived as an altar—flat and covered by a pleated shroud that could double as an altar cloth—underpins a eucharistic interpretation of the sacrifice of Christ, invoking the concomitant theme of the Resurrection. In the upper third, the three Marys arrive on the morning of the third day, carrying ointments to embalm the body of Jesus, which they did not have time to do on Friday evening, since the Sabbath was about to begin. But they found the stone covering the tomb moved aside. An angel sitting on the tomb reminded them of the promise Jesus had made in Galilee—He would rise again after being crucified. In the lower third, the soldiers stationed by the Pharisees to prevent the apostles from stealing the corpse in order to fake a resurrection (Matthew 27: 66) have fallen asleep. Only the slits of their closed eyes can be discerned beneath their coats of mail. Despite a panoply of arrows, spears, and shields, their weapons proved useless.

Illustrations of cloistered life

The cloister-as-sculpted-book contains many other miracles, parables, and apocalyptic subjects impossible to discuss in just a few pages. All of these subjects were designed to encourage meditation by monks or canons, and to trigger multiple associations through the play of spiritual meanings. Literally, Daniel in the Lions' Den was a miraculous incident in the life of the prophet; typologically (or allegorically), it prefigured Christ's Descent into Hell; anagogically, it promised an eschatological victory over Evil; morally— in a meaning more closely related to man's faith and psychological situation—it evoked the anguish experienced by the faithful. In the eyes of the residents of a cloister, then, certain sculptures functioned as a direct allusion to their calling, their religious station, their cloistered life.

Although Benedict and Augustine, the famous compilers of monastic rules, were sometimes depicted, it was the figures of apostles that featured most significantly. The apostles constituted a special model for all communal lifestyles. At Moissac, they are arranged on the corner piers, paired according to canonical tradition— Peter and Paul, James and John, Andrew and Philip, Simon, Bartholomew, and Matthew. Abbot Durand, the Cluniac reformer of Moissac, is set in their midst. At Arles, at Saint-Sauveur in Aix-en-Provence, and at Saint-Bertrand-de-Comminges, they are also distributed individually at the corners or middle of each gallery, accompanied by the abbey's patron saint (such as Trophime and Stephen at Arles). Not all the apostles are depicted, and sometimes only Peter is shown; this Saint Peter of the cloisters stands less for the specific papal figure than for the entire group of disciples that Christ appointed him to lead.

Despite appearances, a certain conceptual unity runs from the figurative reliefs at Moissac to the historiated piers at Silos. For instance, the apostles are always depicted. The sculptors at Silos assembled them into a college, alluding to the first community at Jerusalem, the one that inspired the "true apostolic life" that monks sought to attain. The northwest pier, meanwhile, combines the Road to Emmaus with Doubting Thomas. Reported in two different gospels (Luke 24: 13-35 for Emmaus, John 20: 24–29 for Thomas), the two incidents took place one week apart. On the day of the Resurrection, two disciples (one of whom was named Cleopas) walked toward the village of Emmaus, distraught by recent events. They met a stranger on the way, whom they did not recognize until they were seated at a table with him. Once he broke and blessed the bread, they realized he was Jesus, who then vanished before their eyes. The two men raced back to Jerusalem to inform the apostles. That same evening Jesus appeared to his gathered disciples and showed them his stigmata. But Thomas, who had not been there, refused to believe their story. Eight days later, Jesus appeared again and said to Thomas, "Put your fingers here, and see my hands; and put out your hand, and place it in my side; do not be faithless, but believing." At Silos, the Road to Emmaus and Doubting Thomas are handled as examples of "blindness." The sculptors decided to depict the moment when Christ, about to continue on his way (perhaps around the other side of the pier), is convinced by the two disciples to halt and stay for supper (p. 165). They have not yet recognized him; he is just one pilgrim among others, wearing a ribbed cap and a pouch blazoned with the shell of Compostela. Similarly, Thomas, who is poking his finger between Christ's two ribs, has not yet seen or believed (p. 175). In contrast, his fellow disciples, who remain indifferent to his gesture, have known for a week.

At Silos, these incidents are ascribed directly to the apostles, even when that means distorting the text. Although Cleopas and his companion are simple disciples of Jesus, they are given the book, halo, and bare feet that promotes them to the rank of apostle, just as the group around Thomas is enlarged to include Saint Paul, who obviously could not have witnessed the scene. Here, emblematic impact is more important than textual accuracy. Thanks to Paul, the apostles once again symbolically numbered twelve after having fallen to eleven following the defection of Judas. Paul, Peter, and Andrew take their place in the first row, identified by the name carved on their haloes. Peter holds keys, Andrew the traditional book of the apostles, and Paul a scroll with the following inscription: *Ne magnitudo revelationum extollat me* ("May the grandeur of these revelations not exalt me [above others].") The text on the scroll is an incitement not to break the unity so crucial to the cenobitic world. An identical principle operates in the reliefs of Ascension and Pentecost on the southeast pier, where the apostolic college is featured once again. The upper arches leave room only for the head of Christ (Ascension) or the divine hand (Pentecost). The former disappears into the clouds, the latter emerges from them. The clouds of the Ascension are handled like the waters of the River Jordan in the iconography of baptism, and two angels draw them back almost like a sheet. The same angels lower them in the opposite

WASHING THE DISCIPLES' FEET, CAPITAL, MOISSAC (FRANCE).

direction on Pentecost. Squeezed into two rows, the Twelve Apostles take up some three-quarters of the composition (p. 179). They are joined by Mary, which neither the gospel of Luke nor the Acts of the Apostles mention as being present, although the Acts point out that Mary prayed assiduously with the apostles (Acts 1:14). Iconographic tradition has nevertheless always represented these scenes in this way. Peter and John flank Mary in the Ascension, while in the Pentecost scene her head rises above the compact group in order to be the first to receive the Holy Spirit.

History, Allegory, Whimsy

Already rich in meaning, these biblical themes were joined by many individual capitals whose subject-matter was derived from antique sources, from chansons de geste (epic poems), or from local legends. To take just three cloisters, Arles, Aix, and Moissac all have capitals that might be called historical, featuring figures such as Alexander, Constantine, and Charlemagne. The figure of Alexander the Great enjoyed renewed literary favor starting in the eleventh century, encouraged by the famous *Romance of Alexander*. Having become a fabled hero, the Macedonian king entered the cloister at the head of a procession of freakish animals, Amazons, and sirens from Greece and places eastward. At Moissac, the next-to-last capital in the west gallery depicts an ascension of Alexander who clings to two griffins on his rise to heaven, from which he descended seven days later (p. 43). But should this image be viewed as the intrusion of a secular repertoire into the cloister, or as a moral scene castigating ephemeral power and knowledge, or as a curse against the blasphemous ascension of a pagan anti-Christ?

At Aix and Arles, Constantine was shown upon his horse. Perhaps he merited access to the cloister as the first Christian emperor, perhaps he alludes to the area's imperial past, or perhaps he offers some moral lesson. As for Charlemagne, three capitals at Arles report how he sentenced three barons to hang for having struck Archbishop Turpin. Thanks to the intercession of Saint

<small>THE ASCENSION OF ALEXANDER, CAPITAL, MOISSAC (FRANCE).</small>

Trophime, however, they survived the execution without dying and were ultimately pardoned. Here, the presence of Charlemagne is clearly designed to reinforce the historical authenticity of the local legend of Saint Trophime.

Moralizing interpretations probably played a major role in the sculpted depiction of certain animals, such as a seductive siren whose charms led only to a fish tail, a devoted pelican who sacrificed its life for its offspring, a lion cub who appeared to be dead for three days following its birth until it was "resurrected," and so on. Such animals contributed to the medieval popularity of bestiaries, based on the second-century Greek text, *Physiologus*, and they skillfully combined zoomorphism, religion, and morality. However, the beholder is sometimes confronted with simple birds or deformed monsters that have nothing to do with a moralizing bestiary. At Silos, two large birds are carved face to face, their wings caught in the sinuous branches of a tree (p. 147). Their necks entwine gently, and each pinches the wing of the other in its beak. Given the absence of any literary allusion, perhaps they have no role other than to stress the structure of the capital and contribute to the "beautiful deformity and deformed beauty" described by Saint Bernard.

INTERNAL LOGIC?

Any overall examination of the capitals in a cloister runs up against their irregular distribution and lack of thematic unity. Take, for example, the east gallery of Saint-Pierre in Moissac. Progressing from south to north, a series of capitals shows: Samson wrestling with the lion, then wielding the ass's jawbone; the martyrdoms of Peter and Paul; foliage; Adam and Eve (Temptation, Expulsion, Labor); more foliage; the martyrdom of Saint Laurence, roasted on a gridiron; the Washing of the Disciples' Feet; more foliage; the parable of Lazarus and the Rich Man; dragons; Abbot Durand on the pier; dragons and figures; the Marriage at Cana; still more foliage; the Adoration of the Magi, followed by the Massacre of Innocents; another foliate capital; the martyrdom of Saturninus dragged by a bull; more foliage; the martyrdom of three Spanish saints by burning; the Annunciation and Visitation. Any narrative discourse is therefore interrupted by ornamental carving, and sources of diverse origin are interspersed—Genesis, the gospel of Luke, parables, the Acts of the Apostles, ancient and local martyrologies. The application of typological, moral, or anagogical meanings is hardly more revealing for having linked, for example, the Marriage at Cana to the Adoration of the Magi, or the Annunciation to the three Spanish saints burned alive, and so on.

This anarchic arrangement cannot be explained, therefore—not, at least, by current literary and discursive criteria. In places, the rudiments of an iconographic scheme surface, valid over several capitals in a row, but the existence of a global scheme poses a real problem. And yet twelfth- and thirteenth-century building designers, at least among learned circles, have demonstrated their ability to apply a rational order to overall schemes. For instance, highly refined correspondences govern—on both global and detailed levels—the enameling of the Stavelot portable altar (circa 1150), the right door of the royal portal at Chartres (the Virgin as Seat of Wisdom), and the typological stained glass of the Good Samaritan in Bourges (circa 1210–1215). Cloisters, however, continued to be dominated by discontinuity and profusion, which even seem to have been valued as aesthetic criteria in themselves. Like a literary text, the iconographic text of a cloister demonstrated *varitas*, advocated by classical rhetoric for its stimulating and tonic effect on the spirit, its shimmering and seductive appeal to the ear, and its property of persuasion over heart and mind. Advocating *varitas* does not, however, mean promoting an aesthetics of disorder; it points to another kind of order, whose criteria are not as obvious as discursive rationality. A few elements are given below.

Topographical readings

Topographical interpretation helps to explain the link between the precise location of a capital and its sculpted subject. This can be seen in the ubiquitous cloister theme of the Washing of the Disciples' Feet. As mentioned above, the Benedictine Rule requires the brothers on weekly kitchen duty to wash the other monks' feet every Saturday (RB 35: 7–9); the washing is done by the brother about to complete his weekly duty, along with the one about to begin, as a ritual transfer of responsibility. This humble gesture was clearly perceived not only as a reminder of Christ's own act on Maundy Thursday, but also as a renewal of the apostolic model of communal life. During the Holy Week, certain Cluniac monasteries extended the ceremony to lay people who were ushered into the cloister. The ablutions took place either in the cloister or in the chapter-house. There is reason to believe that it took place near the capital depicting the Washing of the Disciples' Feet, invested with a ritual function on that occasion. Even when the foot-washing scene was part of an Easter cycle—preceded, for example, by Christ's entry into Jerusalem and followed by the Last Supper—its illustration was not an arbitrary iconographic decision, as often confirmed by the precise placing of the depiction. At Silos, it is set on the inner side of the capital, facing the gallery (whereas the Last Supper faces the courtyard), so that the ceremony could conveniently take place in front of the sculpture. Better still, at Saint-Trophime in Arles, it is next to the well, thereby allying the source of water with the perfect prototype of the ceremony.

The cloister of Monreale in Sicily lends itself to topographical analysis of a different sort. Just as the circular architecture of the church of the Holy Sepulcher in Jerusalem provided the West with a powerful model for centrally planned churches (from the palace chapel in Aix to baptisteries everywhere), so the "portico of Solomon" (described in ancient texts as "the cloister of the temple of Solomon") could be ideally copied and metaphorically evoked at Monreale. The cloister's seventeen historiated capitals are placed erratically along all four sides, in no apparent order. But their arrangement attempts to recreate visually, in the space of the quadrangle, a kind of abridged biblical geography as seen from the Holy Land. The east gallery, the presumed direction of the Garden of Eden, is where the capital showing Adam and Eve is found. The northeast corner, turned toward a transposed Bethlehem, contains the Nativity, while not far away are the stories of Samson, which took place at Gaza. The capital of Jacob, depicting his dream at Bethel, is carved on the northwest corner, while a little further along comes Noah, whose ark went aground on Mount Ararat in Armenia. To the south are concentrated all the capitals dealing with the city of Jerusalem itself: the Presentation at the Temple, the Holy Women at the Tomb, and Pentecost. Admittedly, this idealized map displays occasional lapses—although Egypt is correctly located in the southwest corner where the Flight is depicted, the same country reappears in the middle of the east gallery via the stories of Joseph. And the meeting of Christ and Peter at the gates of Rome ("Quo vadis, Domine?") is shown right next to the Garden of Eden! Despite the partial, incomplete nature of these correspondences, the cloister of Monreale creates a truly exotic change of scene when read in this geographic sense. Like the people of Pisa who brought back clumps of earth from Palestine in order to be able to say that the dead buried at Campo Santo now lay in Holy Land, so the Benedictines of Monreale, in their desire to imitate the apostles as closely as possible, could feel themselves transposed to the lands of the East, to the holy enclosure of the cloister of Jerusalem.

**BIRDS, CAPITAL, MONREALE, SICILY (ITALY).
[P. 47] SAINT PETER, PIER, CLOISTER OF SAINT-SAUVEUR CATHEDRAL, AIX-EN-PROVENCE (FRANCE).**

The rhythm of the heavens

The monk's regulated life was orchestrated around the divine offices, night and day; the ability to tell time was therefore crucial. The required information on time and date could be obtained by observing the constellations and setting up a sundial, or through more empirical methods such as measuring the amount of oil, candle, or sand consumed in an hour. Every abbey charged a monk, or even the abbot himself, with monitoring the time and giving the signal for the start of divine offices, which was especially necessary at night.

A ninth-century manuscript currently held by the Bodleian Library in Oxford describes the use of an astrolabe (*horologium stellare*) to determine the time. The relevance of this text to the iconography of cloisters resides in its practical application, because the various buildings of a quadrangle served as the reference markers for the astrolabe. If a critical examination of the text is to be believed, it was composed in north central France for a local monastery. In the absence of archaeological or toponymic confirmation, several places of origin have been proposed: the abbey of Fleury (now Saint-Benoît-sur-Loire), Corbion or Saint-Père in the diocese of Chartres, or perhaps the abbey of Saint-Lomer in Blois (rebuilt between 1128 and 1186). Of course, the system of reference points cited in the document was valid only for the abbey where the manuscript originated, because dependent on latitude, orientation, arrangement of the buildings, and year of composition. But there is no doubt that many other monasteries used similar systems, adapted to their own topography, in order to count the hours.

In the manuscript in question, two contiguous sides of a cloister—the dormitory wing and the refectory wing—serve as clock dial. The time is deduced from the position of constellations in relation to the row of windows in the two wings. For example, "The day of our Lord's Nativity, when you see Gemini located almost above the dormitory and the sign of Orion above the All Saints' chapel, prepare to ring the bells." Or again, "On our Lord's Circumcision, when you see the bright star in the knee of Artophylax placed between the first and second windows of the dormitory, almost at the peak of the roof, then go light the lamps." The entire year was covered by twenty dates corresponding to solemn feasts, both monastic and local, which entailed long blank periods. The first sequences, for instance, included Christmas, Circumcision (January 1), Saint Lomer, Saint Agnes, and the Conversion of Saint Paul (January 19, 21, and 25—identical astronomical position), Saint Sebastian (January 20) and Saint Vincent (January 22), the Presentation in the Temple (February 2), Saint Benedict (March 21), the birth of John the Baptist (June 24), Saints Peter and Paul (June 29), and so on. In every case it was a question of ringing the bells or lighting the lamps for Vigils. The manuscript points out that over the year the observer in the cloister would have to move slightly from the bush in the center of the courtyard toward the well in order to remain aligned with the windows.

Here we see the cloister transformed into a giant astrolabe, with windows serving as markers. Since the columns of the galleries extend below the windows, might the iconography of the sculptures on them correspond to astronomical reference points? It is impossible to test this theory iconographically, since the cloister for which the manuscript was written remains unidentified. The manuscript's stellar clock was intended to function at night, but this analytical system could be converted into daytime equivalents. The observation of constellations could easily be replaced, in daytime, by the rays of the sun. In a diurnal system of solar measurement, columns would provide reference marks of great precision, and two contiguous galleries could function as the arc of a sundial.

Proceeding by analogy, parallels might be established between the list of feasts in the manuscript and the sequential organization of the capitals. Thus a series of capitals with no thematic coherence would become meaningful on the hypothesis that the architectural features of the cloister served as reference marks for a stellar or solar dial. Apparent incoherence may in fact reflect a sequences of feasts on the astronomical calendar. The depiction of certain signs of the zodiac (which are first of all constellations, such as Sagittarius and Gemini) found along the borders of capitals would tend to confirm this. The irregular grouping of historiated capitals between foliate capitals might then correspond to gaps in the festive calendar noted in the manuscript, with a dense cluster of feasts at the end of January, followed by a three-month period of no ceremony between the feasts of Saint Benedict and Saint John the Baptist.

To a cloister's countless roles could then be added that of a clock of stone. Its windows and columns function as features that mark the passage of time. Its capitals etch into stone the memory of the days and times of celebrations. Behind the discontinuity and thematic multiplicity of the sculpture, then, there surfaces the coherent implication of an empirical use of this highly regular space.

Parataxis and citations

The scenes on Romanesque capitals succeed one another with no unifying thread or narrative link—instead, they proceed by juxtaposition, accumulation, indeed repetition. This arrangement evokes the literary device of direct juxtaposition, which goes by the rhetorical name of parataxis. This method of writing was widespread throughout all medieval literary genres from epic poetry to spiritual literature. For the residents of a cloister, the most familiar text was once again the Latin Vulgate Bible. The tale of creation is perhaps the most famous example of paratactic writing: "*And* darkness was upon the face of the deep; *and* the Spirit of

God was moving over the face of the waters. *And* God said, 'Let there be light'; *and* there was light. *And* God saw that the light was good; *and* God separated the light from the darkness." (Genesis 1: 2–5). In many passages of the Vulgate, Saint Jerome abandoned classical Latin's tendency to subordinate clauses with temporal or causal connectors such as *postquam* or *cum* ("as soon as," "while") and simply employed straightforward parataxis using just *et* ("and").

Although words and imagery represent two distinct categories of expression, the validity of parataxis is worth testing on the iconographical text of a cloister. The complexity of this intellectual mechanism can be demonstrated by employing literary examples whose overall features can be transposed onto a "reading" of a cloister. Spiritual treatises, whose edifying role and Biblical references were specifically adapted to the cloister milieu will therefore serve as points of comparison.

Take the writing methods displayed by a chapter of *De disciplina claustrali* (On Cloister Discipline) by Abbot Peter of Celle (died 1183). This chapter discusses the attitude that should be adopted by a good monk. For example, "In no way will he lift his head high, nor go about with a straight neck. Like Rebekah, he shall cover his face from the sight of God with a veil of modesty and humility. . . . He shall not go about like the impious, in circles along paths of vanity and curiosity, but like the angels he shall climb Jacob's ladder, with spirit outreached." Each of these propositions is double, first making an affirmation then citing a biblical example (Genesis 24: 65 and 28:12); ignoring that duality would leave nothing other than a series of citations with no link between them. Celle's text continues with sins (recalling that it was allowed and even recommended that brothers mutually accuse one another): "If a monk accuses a brother for a manifest error, may he utter these comments with the gentleness of the mild Lamb: 'Judas, would you betray the Son of man with a kiss?' (Luke 22: 48). If he accuses him for a hidden error, may he utter a private reprimand and not a public denunciation. If a powerful man or prelate is involved, he shall resemble Nathan before David or the two sons of Noah (II Samuel 12 and Genesis 9: 23): the former, with caution and by indirect paths, circumvented the lion in his way, so well that he caught in his net the most powerful king, by using more skill than severity; as to the latter, they did not want to see the nudity of their father whom they had to revere. . . ."

Once again, the passage is built around two elements, a recommendation and a biblical allusion. But citing the Bible is not merely designed to embellish the argument, something the author could have omitted, for it is simultaneously presented as the motivation behind the recommendation, imbuing it with all its force. The citations are a fundamental element of qualitative style, generating resonances, stimulating images, in short contributing to *varitas*. Allusions and quotations are autonomous elements of the author's argument, constituting a coherent text in counterpoint to his analysis. But if they are merely taken on their own, they seem to follow one another without coherence or connection. They simply become a juxtaposition of diverse allusions, a parataxis of citations.

We can see how Peter of Celle's text might translate into the sculpture of a cloister: a capital showing Noah's drunkenness, the Reproaches of Nathan, the Arrest in Bethany, the Dream of Jacob. For Rebekah, the more traditional scene of Rebekah at the well might have sufficed to allude to her marriage with Isaac and her modest gesture of veiling herself. Such a series of capitals would ultimately form a coherent iconographical text if viewed in counterpoint to another text—a parataxis of capitals.

Excerpts from twenty or more texts could be used to illustrate the same compositional device. But to end with just one, Hugo de Folieto's *De claustro animae* cites examples that correspond to commonly depicted subjects. Discussing unacceptable noise in the cloister and the overly frivolous subjects of the brothers' conversations, Hugo concludes his comments by citing three characters—the Amalekite, the queen of Sheba, and Mary the sister of Martha and Lazarus—who represent three approaches to speech. The Amalekite who reported to David that he had killed Saul ended up like his victim (II Samuel 1); word of Salomon's reputation made the queen of Sheba arrive from faraway Arabia (I Kings 10); Mary, sitting at the Lord's feet, listened to his words instead of helping to serve (Luke 10:39). The first was an example of chatter that leads to downfall, the second an example of reliable report (that required verification), while the third represented the "best portion," namely silence and contemplation.

Three traditional iconographical subjects correspond to these scenes: the execution of Saul's killer; the Queen of Sheba, and Mary's iconographic attribute, namely her anointing of Jesus's feet at Bethany (John 12:3), which sanctions her propensity for contemplation. Hugo's comments confirm that, in his eyes, what counts in an image is less the circumstantial detail than the essential, profound significance.

For a beholder today, three capitals on these subjects would seem to add up to nothing but haphazard juxtaposition. Today's literary and intellectual habits render us insensitive to the richness of parataxis in historiated cloisters. Does that mean a cloister's visual program served as counterpoint to a specific text? Taking the paratactic approach to a logical conclusion, it should be obvious that there was no sole and unique plan, but rather a series of programmatic and iconographic texts that could themselves be juxtaposed. It remains to be determined, in each case, how they are organized and the spiritual meaning behind them—literal, typological, moral, or anagogical. Seen from this standpoint, the *varitas* of a cloister offers a wonderful framework of meaning.

A WORLD ENCLOSED

PRECEDING PAGES: ROMANESQUE GRILLE, CATHEDRAL
CLOISTER, LE PUY (FRANCE).

ABOVE: SANTA MARÍA DE RIPOLL (SPAIN).

Above: VERUELA (SPAIN).
Right: SAN ESTEBAN, SALAMANCA (SPAIN).

PRECEDING PAGES:
SANTA MARÍA DE POBLET (SPAIN).
FOUNTAIN, VALMAGNE (FRANCE).

ABOVE, LEFT TO RIGHT:
WELL, SAINT-TROPHIME, ARLES (FRANCE).
LAVABO, BATALHA (PORTUGAL).
LAVABO, ALCOBAÇA (PORTUGAL).
LAVABO, LE THORONET (FRANCE).

LEFT: Santa María de Ripoll (Spain).
ABOVE: Évora (Portugal).

Left: Tomar (Portugal).
Above: Santi Quattro Coronati, Rome (Italy)

ABOVE: AUGUSTINS, TOULOUSE (FRANCE).

FOLLOWING PAGES:
CATHEDRAL CLOISTER, LE PUY (FRANCE).
MONT-SAINT-MICHEL (FRANCE).

ABOVE, LEFT TO RIGHT:
CADOUIN (FRANCE).
CATHEDRAL CLOISTER, PORTO (PORTUGAL).
BASILICA OF SAN PAOLO FUORI LE MURA, ROME (ITALY).
SAN JUAN DE DUERO (SPAIN).

FOLLOWING PAGES:
TOP: SÉNANQUE (FRANCE).
BOTTOM: LA OLIVA (SPAIN).

Abbaye de Sénanque, Vaucluse, France.

ABBAYE DE SÉNANQUE, VAUCLUSE, FRANCE.

ABOVE: LE THORONET (FRANCE).
RIGHT: REFECTORY ENTRANCE, SANTA MARÍA HUERTA
(SPAIN).

FOLLOWING PAGES: CARTHUSIAN CLOISTER, VILLEFRANCHE-
DE-ROUERGUE (FRANCE).

LEFT: SANTA MARÍA DE POBLET (SPAIN).
ABOVE: GATE TO CARTHUSIAN CLOISTER,
VILLEFRANCHE-DE-ROUERGUE (FRANCE).

FOLLOWING PAGES: CANTERBURY (ENGLAND).

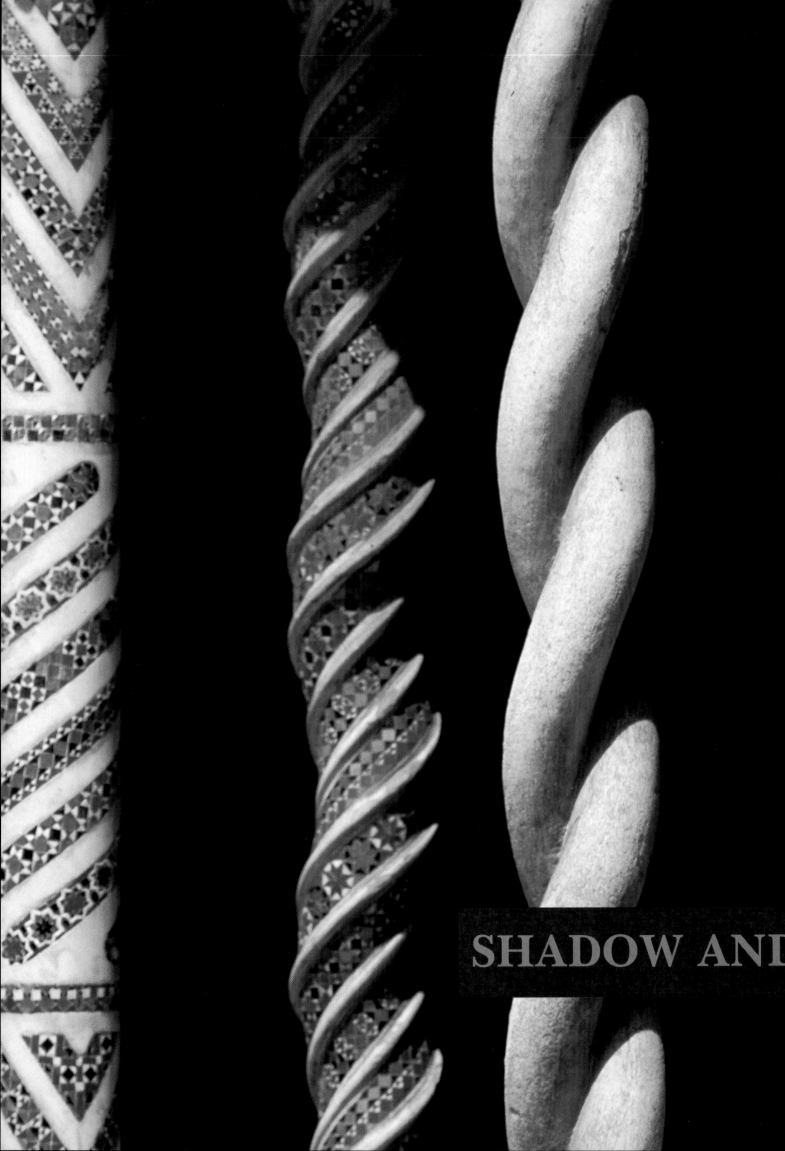

SHADOW AND

COLOR

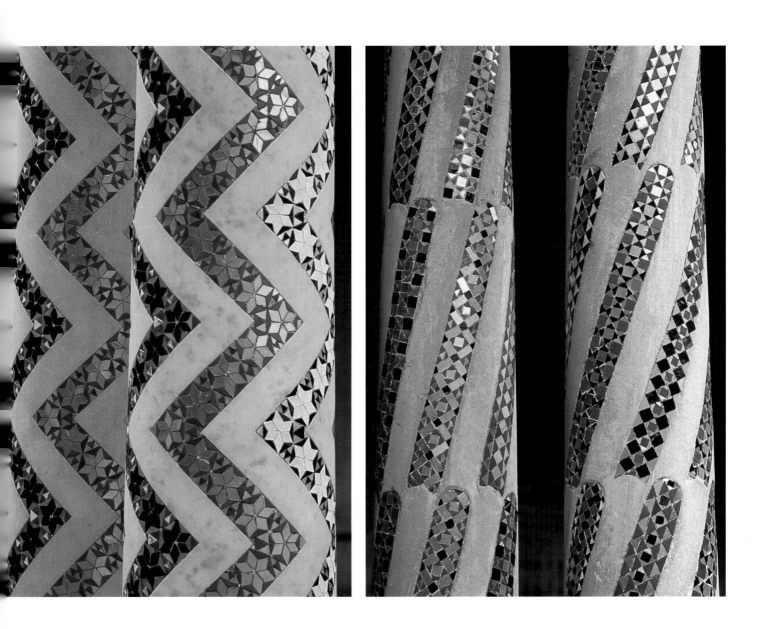

PRECEDING PAGES: **BASILICA OF SAN PAOLO FUORI LE MURA, ROME (ITALY).**
ABOVE: **MOSAIC COLUMNS (DETAILS), MONREALE, SICILY (ITALY).**
RIGHT: **BASILICA OF SAINT JOHN LATERAN, ROME (ITALY).**

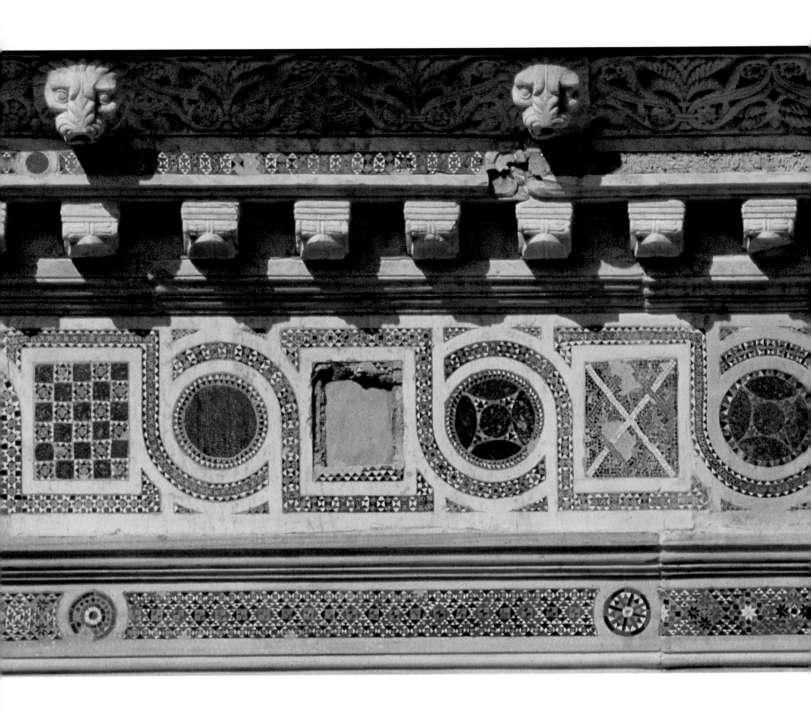

ABOVE: MOSAIC ON THE ARCHITRAVE, BASILICA OF SAN
PAOLO FUORI LE MURA, ROME (ITALY).

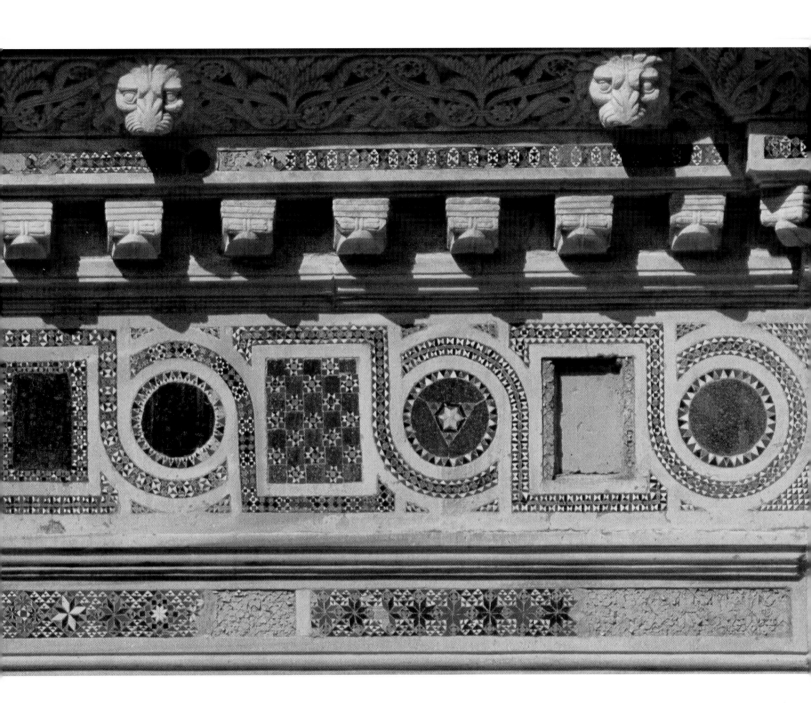

FOLLOWING PAGES: S<small>AN</small> C<small>UGAT DEL</small> V<small>ALLÈS</small> (S<small>PAIN</small>).

85

ABOVE AND RIGHT: SÉNANQUE (FRANCE).
FOLLOWING PAGES: FONTENAY (FRANCE).

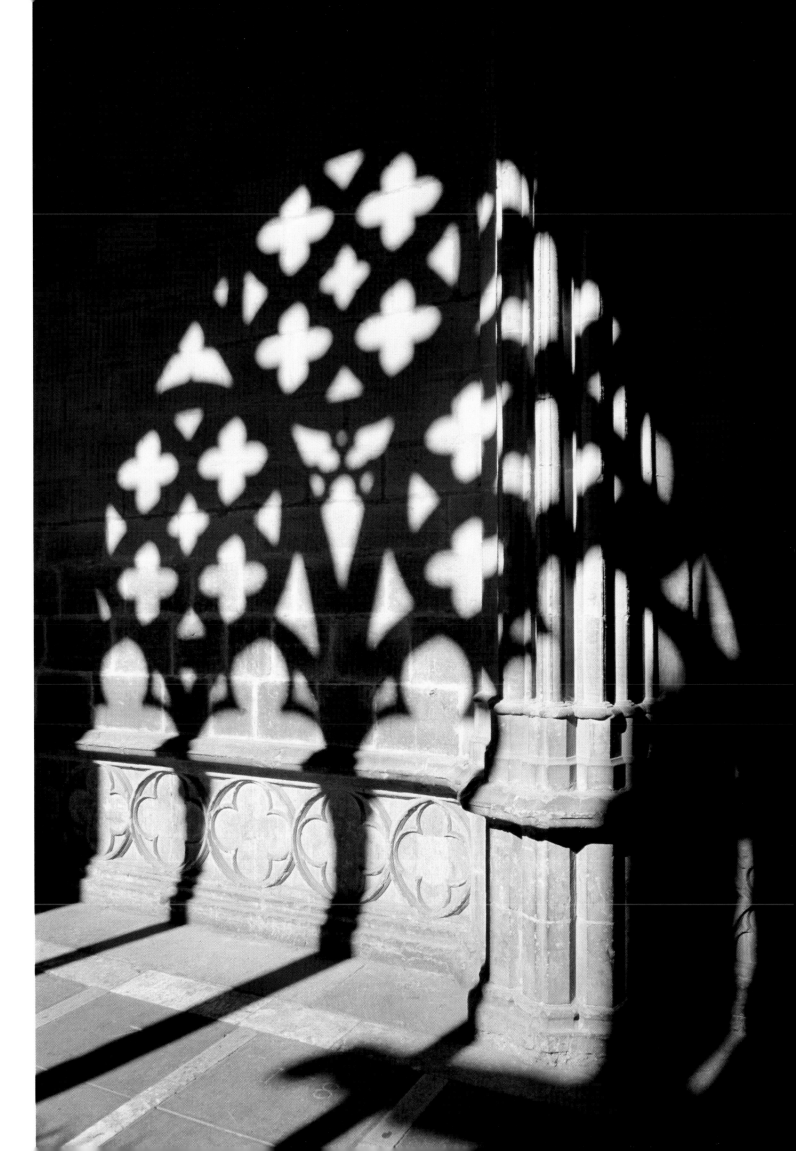

ABOVE, LEFT TO RIGHT:
CLOISTER OF SAINT-SAUVEUR CATHEDRAL, AIX-EN-
PROVENCE (FRANCE).
CATHEDRAL CLOISTER, LE PUY (FRANCE).

MONREALE, SICILY (ITALY).
CATHEDRAL CLOISTER, LE PUY (FRANCE).

UPPER GALLERY (*ABOVE*) AND CEILING (*RIGHT*), SAN JUAN DE
LOS REYES, TOLEDO (SPAIN).

MAJOLICA TILES, SANTA CHIARA, NAPLES (ITALY).

ABOVE AND RIGHT: AZULEJO TILES, CATHEDRAL CLOISTER,
PORTO (PORTUGAL).
FOLLOWING PAGES: MONT-SAINT-MICHEL (FRANCE).

SCULPTED

GARDENS

ABOVE AND RIGHT:
BATALHA (PORTUGAL).
MONREALE, SICILY (ITALY).
BATALHA (PORTUGAL).
FOLLOWING PAGES: MONT-SAINT-MICHEL (FRANCE).

ABOVE: Cathedral cloister, León (Spain).
RIGHT: Jéronimos, Belém (Portugal).

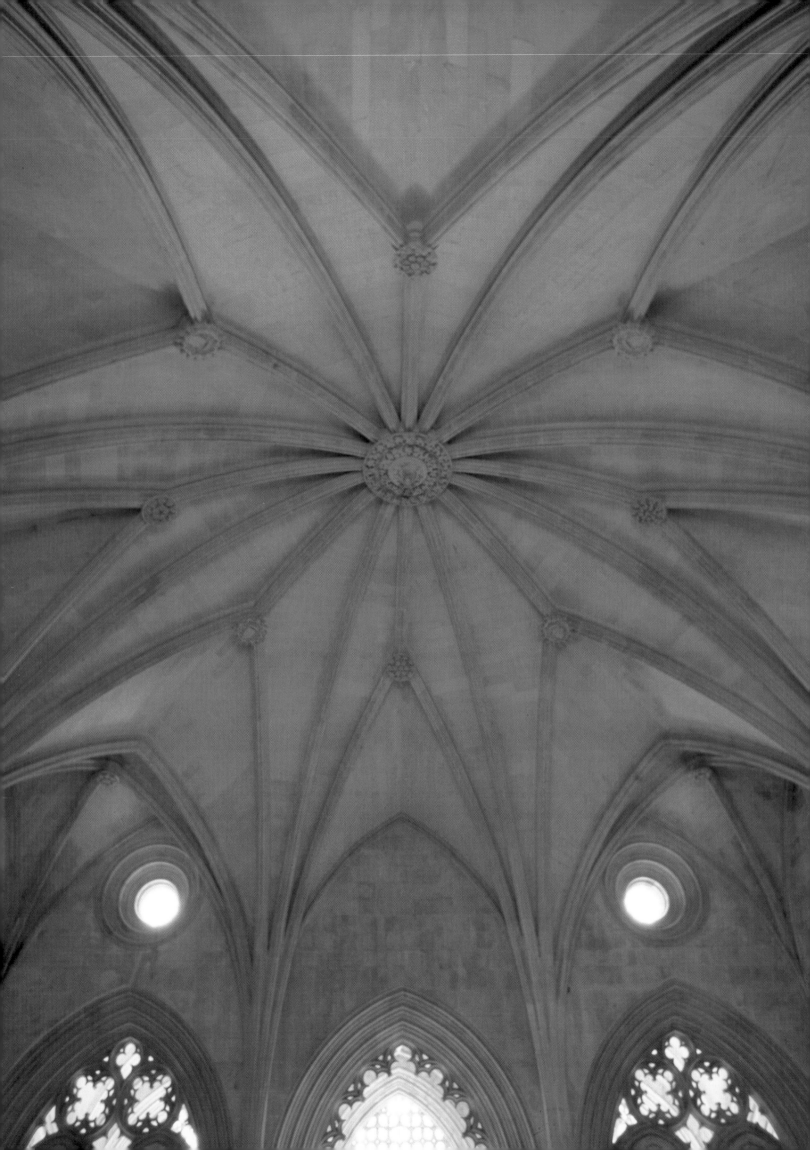

LEFT: VAULT OF CHAPTER-HOUSE, BATALHA (PORTUGAL).
ABOVE, LEFT: VAULT OF FORMER CLOISTER, CONDOM (FRANCE).
ABOVE, RIGHT: FAN VAULT, GLOUCESTER (ENGLAND).
FOLLOWING PAGES: CHAPTER-HOUSE, SANTES CREUS (SPAIN).

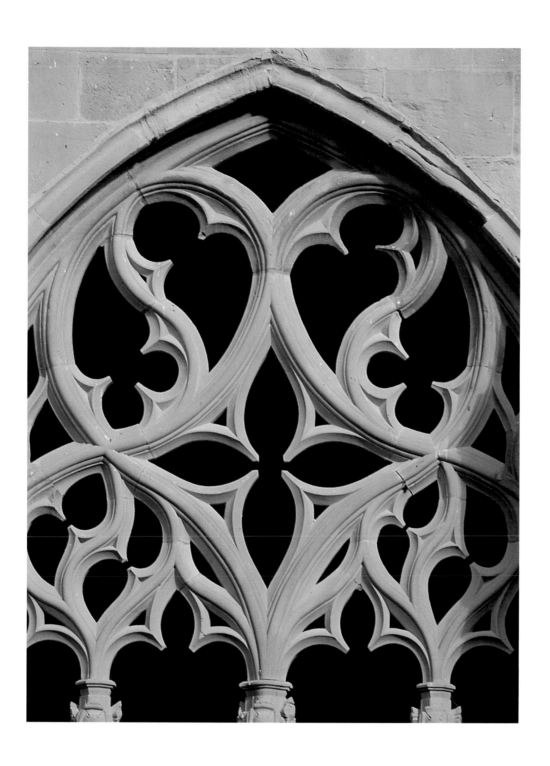

ABOVE: SHAFTS OF COLUMNS, ELNE (FRANCE).
RIGHT: STAIRWAY, TOMAR (PORTUGAL).
FOLLOWING PAGES:
CAPITALS, UPPER GALLERY, SANTO DOMINGO DE SILOS (SPAIN).

ABOVE AND RIGHT: DETAILS OF CAPITALS, SANTO DOMINGO DE SILOS (SPAIN).

ABOVE: **DETAILS OF CAPITALS, SANTO DOMINGO DE SILOS (SPAIN).**
RIGHT: **SCULPTED CAPITAL, MONREALE, SICILY (ITALY).**

136

FIGURES

AND TALES

ABOVE: ADAM AND EVE CARVED ON SPANDREL, SAN PAOLO FUORI
LE MURA, ROME (ITALY).
RIGHT: ADAM AND EVE ON CAPITAL, MONREALE, SICILY (ITALY).

ABOVE: Signs of the Zodiac on the columns of the fountain, Monreale, Sicily (Italy).

FOLLOWING PAGES: DETAILS ON CAPITALS (MOUNTAIN GOATS
AND BIRDS), SANTO DOMINGO DE SILOS (SPAIN).

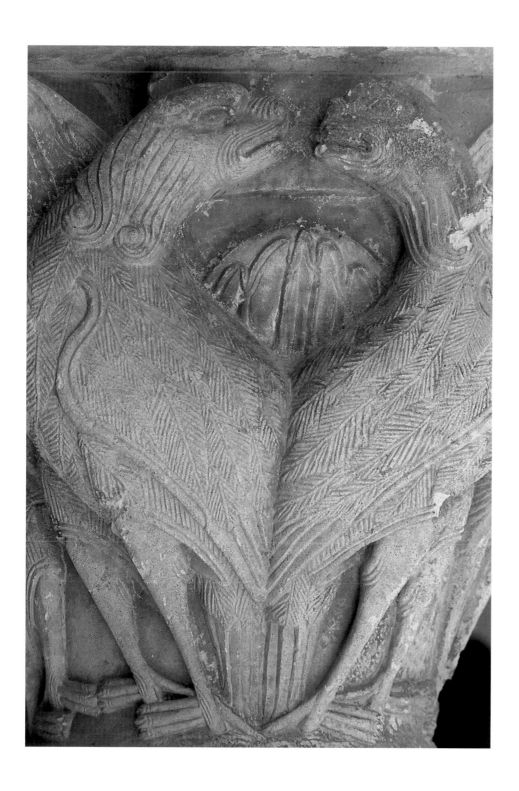

ABOVE AND RIGHT: CAPITALS WITH FANTASTIC FIGURES, LAS
DUEÑAS, SALAMANCA (SPAIN).

ABOVE AND RIGHT: FANTASTIC FIGURES, SANTA CREUS
(SPAIN).

FOLLOWING PAGES: Carved capitals, Monreale, Sicily (Italy).

Above: Samson in Gaza, carved capital, Monreale,
Sicily (Italy).
Right: William II presenting the cathedral to the
Virgin, Monreale, Sicily (Italy).

161

ABOVE: PIER AND ARCADE WITH CARVED CAPITALS, SANTO
DOMINGO DE SILOS (SPAIN).
RIGHT: THE ROAD TO EMMAUS, CARVED PIER, SANTO
DOMINGO DE SILOS.
FOLLOWING PAGES: DETAIL OF THE ROAD TO EMMAUS,
SANTO DOMINGO DE SILOS.

LEFT AND ABOVE: DETAILS OF THE ROAD TO EMMAUS,
SANTO DOMINGO DE SILOS.